A Paines Plough and Th

Daughterhood

by Charley Miles

Supported using public funding by
ARTS COUNCIL
ENGLAND

Cyngor Celfyddydau Cymru
Arts Council of Wales

Daughterhood

by Charley Miles

Cast

PAULINE	Charlotte Bate
RACHEL/MUM	Charlotte O'Leary
SCOT/JEZ/SUPPORT WORKER/	Toyin Omari-Kinch
THEO/DOCTOR/	
LOUIE/PROFESSOR/	
TEACHER/DAD	

Production Team

Direction	Stef O'Driscoll
Lighting	Peter Small
Sound & Original Music	Dominic Kennedy
Movement	Annie-Lunnette Deakin-Foster
Movement Associate	Hayley Chilvers
Assistant Director	Janisè Sadik
Lighting Programmer	Tom Davis
Producer for Paines Plough	Sofia Stephanou
Producer for Theatr Clwyd	Nick Stevenson
Company Stage Manager	Rachel Graham
Technical Stage Manager	Wesley Hughes
Costume Supervisor	Alison Hartnell

CHARLEY MILES (Writer)

Charley Miles is a playwright from rural North Yorkshire. She has written plays for the Royal Court, Leeds Playhouse, and Royal Welsh College of Music and Drama. She has been attached to Paines Plough as their Playwright Fellow in 2018 and Leeds Playhouse as their Channel 4 Playwright in Residence in 2017. Her debut play, BLACKTHORN, was a finalist for the Susan Smith Blackburn prize in New York in 2017. Her new play, THERE ARE NO BEGINNINGS, will premiere at Leeds Playhouse, in autumn 2019. She has original television dramas in development with Buccaneer Media, Mam Tor Productions and Entertainment One.

CHARLOTTE BATE (Pauline)

Charlotte Bate trained at The Guildhall School of Music and Drama.

Theatre credits include: BLACKTHORN (West Yorkshire Playhouse/Edinburgh Festival); THE RIVALS (Watermill Theatre); KING LEAR (Orange Tree Theatre); WATERSHIP DOWN (Watermill Theatre); ROMEO AND JULIET (Sheffield Crucible).

Television credits include: CASUALTY (BBC); THE WHITE HOUSE FARM MURDERS (ITV) and PHILIP K. DICK'S ELECTRIC DREAMS (Channel 4).

Radio credits include: DOCTOR WHO THE PRIMEVAL DESIGN.

CHARLOTTE O'LEARY (Rachel/Mum)

Charlotte O'Leary trained at the Royal Welsh College of Music and Drama.

Theatre credits include: ROUNDABOUT 2018 Season directed by Stef O'Driscoll: ISLAND TOWN, STICKS AND STONES, HOW TO SPOT AN ALIEN (Paines Plough/

Theatr Clwyd); UNDER MILK WOOD directed by Brendan O'Hea (Watermill Theatre); HUSH directed by Hannah Bannister (Paines Plough/ RWCMD).

Television credits include: THE WITCHER (Netflix Originals).

Radio credits include: TORCHWOOD directed by Scott Handcock (Big Finish Productions).

TOYIN OMARI-KINCH (Scot/Jez/Support Worker/ Theo/Doctor/Louie/Professor/ Teacher/Dad)

Toyin Omari-Kinch is an established actor who recently played David Taylor for over a year in WAR HORSE at the National Theatre and during a national tour of the production. He and the production received fantastic reviews.

Toyin played the role of Eric the Archer in the RSC and National Theatre of Scotland's US tour of DUNSINANE. The show was adapted by David Greig and directed by Roxana Silbert and went to North Carolina, Washington, Chicago and Los Angeles. He has also appeared in numerous productions for the Birmingham Rep.

On the small screen, he has featured in DOCTORS for the BBC.

STEF O'DRISCOLL (Direction)

Stef O'Driscoll is Artistic Director of nabokov and previously Associate Director at Paines Plough and Lyric Hammersmith.

As director, theatre includes: ISLAND TOWN, STICKS AND STONES, HOW TO SPOT AN ALIEN (Paines Plough/ Theatr Clwyd); WITH A LITTLE BIT OF LUCK, HOPELESSLY DEVOTED (Paines Plough/Birmingham REP/ Latitude); BLISTER (Paines Plough/ RWCMD); LAST NIGHT (nabokov/

Roundhouse); STORYTELLING ARMY (nabokov/Brighton Festival); SLUG (nabokov/Latitude); BOX CLEVER (nabokov); YARD GAL (Ovalhouse); THE UNMASTER, A TALE FROM THE BEDSIT (Roundhouse/Bestival), FINDING HOME (Roundhouse); A GUIDE TO SECOND DATE SEX, WHEN WOMEN WEE (Underbelly/Soho Theatre); A MIDSUMMER NIGHT'S DREAM [co-director] (Lyric Hammersmith).

As Associate Director, theatre includes: MOGADISHU (Lyric Hammersmith/Royal Exchange Theatre, Manchester).

As Assistant Director, theatre includes: WASTED (Paines Plough); HENRY IV (Donmar Warehouse/St Anne's Warehouse, Brooklyn); BLASTED (Lyric Hammersmith).

Upcoming projects include: A HISTORY OF WATER IN THE MIDDLE EAST (Royal Court Theatre); LIT (Nottingham Playhouse/HighTide).

Awards include: WITH A LITTLE BIT OF LUCK (BBC Radio & Music Award for Best Production); YARD GAL (Fringe Report Award for Best Fringe Production).

PETER SMALL (Lighting)
Peter Small is an Offie and Theatre & Technology Award-nominated lighting designer working across theatre, dance and opera. He regularly collaborates with Paines Plough, including lighting productions in their pop-up theatre ROUNDABOUT.

Recent lighting design for theatre includes: RADIO (Arcola Theatre); SQUARE GO (59E59 New York, Francesca Moody Productions); AD LIBIDO (Soho Theatre); YOU STUPID DARKNESS! (Paines Plough/Theatre Royal Plymouth); ROUNDABOUT 2018 Season: HOW TO SPOT AN

ALIEN, STICKS AND STONES and ISLAND TOWN (Paines Plough/Theatr Clwyd); SQUARE GO (Francesca Moody Productions); ROUNDABOUT 2017 Season: OUT OF LOVE, BLACK MOUNTAIN (Offie-nominated) and HOW TO BE A KID (Paines Plough/Theatr Clwyd/Orange Tree Theatre); PLASTIC (Poleroid Theatre/Old Red Lion); OLD FOOLS (Southwark Playhouse); Offie and Theatre & Technology Award-nominated A GIRL IN SCHOOL UNIFORM (WALKS INTO A BAR) (New Diorama); FOX (Old Red Lion); MEMORY OF LEAVES (UK tour); SHE CALLED ME MOTHER (Pitch Lake Productions/UK tour); THE VENUS FACTOR (MTA Academy/Bridewell Theatre); EAST END BOYS AND WEST END GIRLS (Arcola Theatre /tour); A MIDSUMMER NIGHT'S DREAM, FREE ASSOCIATION and CRAZY LADY (Forum Alpbach, Austria); RICHARD III and BARD ON BOARD 2 (Royal Court/Queen Mary 2 Ocean Liner).

Opera and musical theatre include: THE RAPE OF LUCRETIA (Stratford Circus); ALL OR NOTHING (West End/tour); CINDERELLA (Loughborough Theatre); TOM & JERRY (EventBox Theatre, Egypt). Peter was revival lighting designer on KISS ME KATE for Oper Graz.

Upcoming projects include BABY REINDEER, DO OUR BEST at Edinburgh Festival Fringe, SPIDERFLY (Theatre503); LIT (Nottingham Playhouse/HighTide) and taking AD LIBIDO and SQUARE GO on tour.

DOMINIC KENNEDY (Sound & Original Music)
Dominic Kennedy is a sound designer and music producer for performance and live events; he has a keen interest in developing new work and implementing sound and

music at an early stage in a creative process. Dominic is a graduate from Royal Central School of Speech and Drama, where he developed specialist skills in collaborative and devised theatre making, music composition and installation practices. His work often fuses found sound, field recordings, music composition and synthesis.

Recent design credits include: 17 (WILDCARD); YOU STUPID DARKNESS! (Paines Plough/Theatre Royal Plymouth); POP MUSIC (Paines Plough/Birmingham REP/Latitude); SKATE HARD TURN LEFT (Battersea Arts Centre); ROUNDABOUT 2018 SEASON (Paines Plough/Theatr Clwyd); ANGRY ALAN (Soho Theatre); THE ASSASSINATION OF KATIE HOPKINS (Theatr Clwyd); WITH A LITTLE BIT OF LUCK (Paines Plough/BBC Radio 1Xtra); RAMONA TELLS JIM (Bush Theatre); AND THE REST OF ME FLOATS (Outbox); I AM A TREE (Jamie Wood); BOX CLEVER (nabokov).

ANNIE-LUNNETTE DEAKIN-FOSTER (Movement)

Annie-Lunnette Deakin-Foster is a passionate contemporary dance theatre choreographer, maker and movement director and is a co-founding member of award-winning company, C-12 Dance Theatre.

Recent theatre credits include: YOU STUPID DARKNESS! by Sam Steiner, directed by James Grieve (Paines Plough/Theatre Royal Plymouth); GRIMM TALES, Phillip Pullman's collection adapted by Philip Wilson, directed by Kirsty Housley (Unicorn Theatre); JERICHO'S ROSE by Althea Theatre (Hope & Anchor); POP MUSIC by Anna Jordan, directed by James Grieve (Birmingham REP/Barry Jackson tour/Paines Plough national tour); THE COURT MUST HAVE A QUEEN by Ade Solanke,

directed by Sam Curtis Lindsay (Hampton Court Palace); THESE BRIDGES by Phoebe Eclair-Powell (WCYT as part of National Theatre Connections at the Bush); THE LITTLE MATCH GIRL AND OTHER HAPPIER TALES by Joel Horwood and Emma Rice (Shakespeare's Globe/Bristol Old Vic/national tour); THE DARK ROOM by Angela Betzien (Theatre503); I KNOW ALL THE SECRETS OF MY WORLD by Natalie Ibu (tiata fahodzi/national tour).

Recent dance credits include: FORCE (Abbey Road Studios/Imagine Festival Watford/Greenwich & Docklands International Festival/Netherlands); SHHH! (Dance City/MAC Birmingham/Norwich Playhouse/The Woodville Gravesend/CircoMedia Bristol/Winchester Theatre Royal); THE VAN MAN (Watch This Space at the National/St Albans Festival/Freedom Festival Hull/The Albany Outdoors).

JANISÈ SADIK (Assistant Director)

Janisè Sadik is an emerging theatremaker and director. She is Paines Plough's Trainee Director for 2019 and was a part of the Young Vic Directors program and completed her Boris Karloff Foundation in 2017. She has been a co-workshop leader at Park Theatre leading the Creative Learning Programme since 2015 directing the end of term showcase. She's facilitated in various creative buildings such as Hoxton Hall, Lyric Hammersmith, Ovalhouse and Wimbledon College of Arts. In 2018 she set up a Youth Theatre company at We Are Spotlight working with young actors that don't have access to training. She has worked internationally in rural parts of South India to run creative theatre projects with young children to empower and build their confidence. She enjoys work that is experimental, devised and brings new writing to life.

Theatre credits as director include: MILK & OREOS, winner of the Pandora Award 2015, co-written by Janisè Sadik & Seraphina Beh (Melanin Box Festival); BREAKING THE INTERNET (Ovalhouse Summer School 2017); BLURRED LINES (Etcetera Theatre); US by Priscilla Lafayette Kwabi (Camden People's Theatre); HYDRAULIC by Tristan Fynn-Aiduenu (Wimbledon College of Arts).

Film credits as director include: SHE by Andrè James.

RACHEL GRAHAM (Company Stage Manager)
Rachel Graham is a freelance stage manager based in London. She graduated in 2016 with a 1st Class BA (Hons) Stage Management from Rose Bruford College of Theatre and Performance.

Theatre credits include: RAGS (Hope Mill Theatre/Aria Entertainment); CRAZY FOR YOU (Mountview at Pleasance); ROBIN HOOD (Qdos Productions); THE POLITICAL HISTORY Of SMACK AND CRACK (Edinburgh/Soho Theatre/W14 Productions); BLACKTHORN (InSite, Roundabout @ Edinburgh); LONELY PLANET (Trafalgar Studios); NOT TALKING (defibrillator/Arcola Theatre); A NIGHT AT THE OSCARS (Aria Entertainment); ALADDIN (Qdos Productions); WHITE CHRISTMAS (Curtain Call Productions/Crewe Lyceum); 31 HOURS (W14 Productions/Bunker Theatre); SOME LOVERS (Aria Entertainment/The Other Palace); JAM (W14 Productions/Finborough Theatre); POSH (Can't Think Theatre Company/Pleasance Theatre); THE PAJAMA GAME (Urdang Academy at Pleasance Theatre); CINDERELLA (First Family Entertainment); SWEENEY TODD (Royal Academy of Music/Theatre Royal Stratford East); SISTER ACT (Curtain Call Productions/Crewe Lyceum).

PAINES PLOUGH

Paines Plough tours the best new theatre to all four corners of the UK and around the world. Whether you're in Liverpool or Lyme Regis, Brighton or Berwick-Upon-Tweed, a Paines Plough show is coming to a theatre near you soon.

'The lifeblood of the UK's theatre ecosystem' *Guardian*

Paines Plough was formed in 1974 over a pint of Paines Bitter in the Plough pub. Since then we've produced more than 150 new productions by world renowned playwrights like Stephen Jeffreys, Abi Morgan, Sarah Kane, Mark Ravenhill, Dennis Kelly, Mike Bartlett, Kate Tempest and Vinay Patel. We've toured those plays to hundreds of places from Bristol to Belfast to Brisbane.

'That noble company Paines Plough, de facto national theatre of new writing' *Daily Telegraph*

In the past three years we've produced 30 shows and performed them in over 200 places across four continents. We tour to more than 30,000 people a year from Cornwall to the Orkney Islands; in village halls and Off-Broadway, at music festivals and student unions, online and on radio, and in our own pop-up theatre ROUNDABOUT.

Our Programme 2019 premieres the best new British plays touring the length and breadth of the UK in theatres, clubs and pubs everywhere from city centres to seaside towns. ROUNDABOUT hosts a jam-packed Edinburgh Festival Fringe programme and brings mini-festivals to each stop on its nationwide tour. Our COME TO WHERE I'M FROM app features 180 short audio plays available to download free from the App Store and GooglePlay.

'I think some theatre just saved my life' @kate_clement on Twitter

PAINES PLOUGH ◖ ROUNDABOUT

'A beautifully designed masterpiece in engineering' *The Stage*

ROUNDABOUT is Paines Plough's beautiful portable in-the-round theatre. It's a completely self-contained 168-seat auditorium that flat packs into a single lorry and pops up anywhere from theatres to school halls, sports centres, warehouses, car parks and fields.

We built ROUNDABOUT to tour to places that don't have theatres. ROUNDABOUT travels the length and breadth of the UK bringing the nation's best playwrights and a thrilling theatrical experience to audiences everywhere.

Over the last six years ROUNDABOUT has hosted over 2,000 hours of entertainment for more than 100,000 people in places ranging from a churchyard in Salford to Margate seafront.

ROUNDABOUT was designed by Lucy Osborne and Emma Chapman at Studio Three Sixty in collaboration with Charcoalblue and Howard Eaton.

WINNER of Theatre Building of the Year at The Stage Awards 2014

'ROUNDABOUT wins most beautiful interior venue by far @edfringe.'
@ChaoticKirsty on Twitter

'ROUNDABOUT is a beautiful, magical space. Hidden tech make it Turkish-bath-tranquil but with circus-tent-cheek. Aces.'
@evenicol on Twitter

ROUNDABOUT was made possible thanks to the generous support of the following Trusts and individuals and all who named a seat in ROUNDABOUT.

TRUSTS AND FOUNDATIONS
Andrew Lloyd Webber Foundation
Paul Hamlyn Foundation
Garfield Weston Foundation
J Paul Getty Jnr Charitable Trust
John Ellerman Foundation

CORPORATE
Universal Consolidated Group
Howard Eaton Lighting Ltd
Charcoalblue
Avolites Ltd
Factory Settings
Total Solutions

Pop your name on a seat and help us pop-up around the UK:
www.justgiving.com/fundraising/roundaboutauditorium

www.painesplough.com/roundabout
#ROUNDABOUTPP

Paines Plough

Joint Artistic Directors	James Grieve
	George Perrin
Producer	Sofia Stephanou
Finance and Administration Manager	Svetlana Karadimova
Technical Director	Colin Everitt
Assistant Producer	Christabel Holmes
Marketing and Audience Development Officer	Jo Langdon
Production Assistant	Phillippe Cato
Finance and Administration Assistant	Eman Bhatti
Trainee Producer	Nicky Thirugnanam
Trainee Administrator	Adam Poland
Trainee Director	Janisè Sadik
Production and Marketing Placement	Lacey Ruttley
Admin Placement	Ellie Fitz-Gerald
Press Representative	The Corner Shop PR
Graphic Designer	Michael Windsor-Ungureanu
	Thread Design

Board of Directors

Kim Grant (Chair), Ankur Bahl, Nia Janis, Dennis Kelly, Matthew Littleford, Sarah Mansell, Christopher Millard, Cindy Polemis, Carolyn Saunders and Andrea Stark.

Paines Plough Limited is a company limited by guarantee and a registered charity.
Registered Company no: 1165130
Registered Charity no: 267523

Paines Plough, 2nd Floor, 10 Leake Street, London SE1 7NN
+ 44 (0) 20 7240 4533

office@painesplough.com
www.painesplough.com

 Follow @PainesPlough on Twitter

 Like Paines Plough at facebook.com/PainesPloughHQ

 Follow @painesplough on Instagram

Donate to Paines Plough at justgiving.com/PainesPlough

Theatr
Clwyd

The award-winning Theatr Clwyd is Wales' biggest producing theatre.

Based in Flintshire, the gateway to North Wales, since 1976 Theatr Clwyd has been a cultural powerhouse producing world-class theatre, from the UK Theatre Award-winning musical THE ASSASSINATION OF KATIE HOPKINS and National Theatre and West End Olivier award-winning comedy HOME, I'M DARLING, to the site-specific, immersive THE GREAT GATSBY and its sell-out rock 'n' roll pantomime.

Led by Artistic Director Tamara Harvey and Executive Director Liam Evans-Ford, Theatr Clwyd's world-class team of workshop, wardrobe and scenic artists, props makers and technicians ensure the skills vital to a vibrant theatre industry are nurtured right in the heart of Wales. Alongside the three theatre spaces, cinema, café, bar and art galleries, Theatr Clwyd works with the community in many different guises across all art forms and is recognised as a cultural leader for its cross-generational theatre groups, work in youth justice and diverse programme of arts, health and wellbeing.

Find out more: www.theatrclwyd.com
Tweet us: @ClwydTweets
Follow us: Facebook.com/TheatrClwyd

 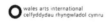

DAUGHTERHOOD

Charley Miles

For Izzy and for Eve

Acknowledgements

All love and thanks to my Paines Plough family: George, James, Sofia, Jo, Chris, Phill, Eman, and all else – for the rock-solid foundation they have given me.

Thanks to Stef O'Driscoll, for the generosity and warmth she brings to everything and that has enabled us all to thrive; to our brilliant cast, Charlie, Charlotte and Toyin, for the depths that they have mined for this play; to Janisè, Annie, Hayley and Rachel, for their contributions to the warmest of rehearsal rooms.

To the rest of the Roundabout family – most especially to my fellow writers, Daf James and Nathan Bryon, for making this job feel bigger, safer, and more joyful.

To my actual family: Mum, Dad, sisters and Frankie, for their enduring tolerance.

To my other constants: on this occasion, most particularly Zoe Kelly and Robbie Fergusson for their early voices of wisdom and encouragement; and, as ever, to Tashan Mehta and Charlotte Salter, for keeping me strong in craft and sane in perspective.

Always thanks to my agent, Marnie Podos – another lioness.

C.M.

Characters

RACHEL
PAULINE
SCOT
JEZ
SUPPORT WORKER (SW)
THEO
DOCTOR
LOUIE
PROFESSOR
TEACHER
DAD
MUM

Note on Play

Rachel and Pauline are sisters.

Nine or ten years between them, depending on the month.

Every third scene takes place in the present, over twenty-four hours. The intervening scenes are two halves of the same moment, moving backwards in time over several years.

The play should feel like a series of mirrored images.

– in place of dialogue denotes an active choice not to speak.

– in between lines of dialogue denotes an unclaimed silence.

This text went to press before the end of rehearsals and so may differ slightly from the play as performed.

*

Rachel and Pauline are twenty-five and thirty-four.
It's a huge gap. Almost insurmountable.
They stand on the mouth of a volcano,
which could erupt at any moment.
They feel it beneath their feet.
Their weight is perfectly balanced
just about maintaining equilibrium
on top of the tectonic plates, to stop them from diverging.
The slightest moment of weight, on either side,
could split the earth between them
and leave a gaping hole.

*

One

RACHEL   Paul!
            Pauliiiiiiiiiiiiine?
            Paul have you got a tenner?? I don't have any cash and
            Alright mate I'm just having an ask!
            Pauline I'm looking for your handbag.
            I've found your handbag.
            I'm removing a tenner…
            Sorry!
            Thank you…!
            …

            –

RACHEL   Hey!
            God what you lurking in the dark for?
            …I'm home!

PAULINE   Yeah I heard.

RACHEL   Sorry I forgot to get some out before I left.
            You don't mind. So used to everything being contactless.

PAULINE   Think half the neighbours heard too.

RACHEL   You missed me…

PAULINE   Not with that entrance.

RACHEL   Come on. It's not that late.
            I grabbed a bottle at King's Cross.

PAULINE   Dad's asleep.

RACHEL   –
            I didn't think.

PAULINE   I waited at the station.

RACHEL   Did you? Didn't see you.

PAULINE	You weren't in on time.
RACHEL	Only twenty minutes.
PAULINE	I had to get back for him.
RACHEL	I tried to call.
PAULINE	I was in the car.
RACHEL	Your mobile?
PAULINE	I left it here.
RACHEL	Kind of defeats the point of a mobile phone right? It's mobile…
PAULINE	–
RACHEL	Hug?
	–
RACHEL	I tried to call an Uber. At the station. When you didn't show up.
PAULINE	How did that go?
RACHEL	Would've been a three-hour wait. How the bastards pull you in. Weird second nature now. Tap tap tap. Whole row of cabs lined up and there I am on my app without even Sorry was I interrupting something?
PAULINE	Just tired. Past my bedtime.
RACHEL	I'll pop the kettle on.
PAULINE	I'll do it.
RACHEL	Okay I'll drop my bags.
PAULINE	Why are you going that way?
RACHEL	My room…
PAULINE	Dad's in there.
RACHEL	Why's he not

PAULINE   Can't manage the stairs.

RACHEL   Oh.
               When did that happen?

PAULINE   I made up the little room for you.

RACHEL   Oh. Thanks / but

PAULINE   Or you can sleep on the zed bed.

RACHEL   Is that still here?? Must be crawling.

PAULINE   Do whatever you like.

RACHEL   –
               I'm sorry about the train Pauline.

PAULINE   Not a problem.

RACHEL   You're looking good.

PAULINE   (*A noise.*)

RACHEL   I like your haircut.

PAULINE   It hasn't been.

RACHEL   It's nice longer. Suits you.

PAULINE   Thanks.
               Yours is
               nice
               too.

RACHEL   Yeah? Been going to a new salon. Had it cut by
               this girl called Fanny le Blanc.

PAULINE   Fanny?

RACHEL   I thought she was just going to be some Essex
               bird with a French manicure but turns out she
               actually is legit Parisian. Says on the website
               she prides herself on her 'French touch'.
               Fanny le Blanc with the French touch.
               I almost pissed myself.
               But it does look good doesn't it?

PAULINE	Very nice. Very French.
	–
RACHEL	It was a fucking
PAULINE	(*Flinch*.)
RACHEL	nightmare of a journey.
PAULINE	It's always bad with the races on.
RACHEL	Yeah.
PAULINE	Stupid girls.
RACHEL	I mean it's the lads more than / anyone else
PAULINE	It's the girls. They're downright aggressive.
RACHEL	Just drunk.
PAULINE	Exactly.
RACHEL	When was the last time you were getting a train on a Saturday night?
PAULINE	–
RACHEL	Tea, did you say?
PAULINE	Yeah not for ages.
RACHEL	D'you have decaf?
PAULINE	What's the point in that?
RACHEL	What?
PAULINE	Have a glass of squash if you want.
RACHEL	You lost me.
PAULINE	Why would you be wasting money on tea that's not tea?
RACHEL	It is tea. Just not caffeinated.
PAULINE	You can have hot squash if you're gonna play fussy / beggars

RACHEL   Oh my God Paul I JUST walked through the door.
            Where do you want me to put my bags?

PAULINE   The little room. I said.

RACHEL   You know that I'm not going to sleep in there.

PAULINE   –

RACHEL   What about Mum and Dad's room?

PAULINE   I'm in there.

RACHEL   What? Why?

PAULINE   Cos it's the biggest.

RACHEL   So that's why you've moved him downstairs is it?
            –
            That was a joke.

PAULINE   –

RACHEL   When did they start putting security guards on the train?

PAULINE   I didn't know they had.

RACHEL   Remember when we did the races for Amy's eighteenth? Didn't she get thrown off that time?

PAULINE   She wasn't thrown off.

RACHEL   You know what I mean.
            Gave me some insight into what it's like to be the sober one for once. No fun if you're not pissed is it.
            Some girl insisted I was in her seat.
            And I was like – no love honestly, I'm on since London.

PAULINE   It's always the girls.

RACHEL   I mean – it's not.

PAULINE   You just said it

RACHEL	This guy was worse That was standing in the vestibule and I had to crush up next to him and he was all breathing down my face and looking in my top He was way worse. Than the girls. Actually.
PAULINE	You wouldn't have had to stand next to him though would you If she hadn't pushed you out your seat.
RACHEL	I s'pose.
PAULINE	So hot squash then?
RACHEL	Normality is fine.
PAULINE	–
RACHEL	I can do it. Normality for you?
PAULINE	Yes. Normal for me thanks.
RACHEL	Normality for you.
PAULINE	I remember Rach it's just not as funny as when we were kids.
RACHEL	–
PAULINE	I'll take your bags up for you.
RACHEL	I can manage.
PAULINE	You're doing the tea.
RACHEL	Where you gonna put them?
PAULINE	In the / little room
RACHEL	Paul – I'm not sleeping in there.
PAULINE	Well look I'm sorry but that's the / room that's
RACHEL	I SAID NO.
PAULINE	Don't you shout at me. If you've woken up Dad
RACHEL	We live in a three-bedroom house Pauline. I will sleep. In another. Room.

PAULINE   Two-bed.

RACHEL   I think I can count.

PAULINE   If you've been counting on
Guesstimating
on a three-bed house then I'm afraid you're
going to be disappointed because actually this
is technically a two-bedroom house with two
reception rooms.

RACHEL   Sorry, what?

PAULINE   That's the dining room.
It's not even supposed to be a bedroom.

RACHEL   I'm sorry why are we fighting about this?

PAULINE   I'm not fighting. I'm just letting you know
for your future plans. For whatever it is you
think you're due.

RACHEL   What is that supposed to mean?

PAULINE   If you'd've given me more notice maybe I'd've
been able to rejig something.

RACHEL   Well I'm sorry my presence is such an
inconvenience.

PAULINE   I never said that. Where are you going?

RACHEL   I'll see you in the morning. Try and remember
to get out the right side tomorrow yeah?

PAULINE   Nice to have you home Rachel.

RACHEL   Delighted to be back.

Two

RACHEL	Fuck I'm nervous. Jesus. Fucking hell. Did not think I would be this nervous.
SCOT	I can tell.
RACHEL	Don't say that!
SCOT	Not in a bad way.
RACHEL	If you can tell I'm nervous, there's nothing in that is a good way.
SCOT	Shows you care.
RACHEL	Yeah but I need to be you know Composed. And I need to have my shit together. Fuck. Look at my hand.
SCOT	I've never heard you swear so much.
RACHEL	God I'm bad. I know I am.
SCOT	Not normally.
RACHEL	I think it's like a thing from my childhood. My dad fucking *hated* us swearing. Like actually hated it. Like when I was eight one time in front of him I accidentally said fart
SCOT	Fart? As in – ?
RACHEL	Yeah as in like fucking whatever it is you call it when it's not a fart.
SCOT	Trump?
RACHEL	On point.
SCOT	Thank you.
RACHEL	We called it a poop. God, why am I talking about this?

SCOT   No go on.

RACHEL   Anyway it just slipped out

SCOT   Your fart?

RACHEL   Huh?

SCOT   Your fart just slipped out?

RACHEL   Funny.

SCOT   Thank you.

RACHEL   It was what people called it at school and
            I wasn't going to go around being like WHO
            POOPED all the time when everyone else was
            saying fart.

SCOT   Social suicide.

RACHEL   I swear to God
            He did not speak to me
            For a month.

SCOT   No…

RACHEL   I shit you not.

SCOT   Your da still hates it?

RACHEL   He actually got over it, eventually.
            It's my sister still hates it.

SCOT   How old's your sister?

RACHEL   Nine years. Older.

SCOT   That's a big gap.

RACHEL   Yeah it is quite.

SCOT   –
            Your hand's stopped shaking.

RACHEL   Oh yeah.
            Thanks.

SCOT   For what?

RACHEL	Distracting me. Being here.
SCOT	We're all in this together.
RACHEL	I don't want to let you down.
SCOT	As if you could let anyone down.
RACHEL	– Scot, do you want to grab a drink? After.
SCOT	Um
RACHEL	You know just talk it all through how it went and stuff.
SCOT	Yeah sure. We should do that.
RACHEL	It'd be nice to you know Chat more. When we're not You know Waiting to go into Parliament.
SCOT	It's not exactly low-pressure stuff.
RACHEL	Nope.
SCOT	Not to make you nervous again.
RACHEL	I'm not nervous any more.
SCOT	–
RACHEL	Will you be hungry after, do you reckon?
SCOT	I don't know.
RACHEL	We could grab dinner.
SCOT	Yeah maybe.
RACHEL	Beer and a burger. Just something chill.
SCOT	Rachel…
RACHEL	What?

SCOT   I'm not good at coy.

RACHEL   Who's being coy?

SCOT   I mean you're not – not successfully.

RACHEL   (*Laughs*.)

SCOT   I just mean that if you're expecting me to be
            coy in return
            I'm not good at that.

RACHEL   Okay.

SCOT   –
            I've probably got to get back after.

RACHEL   I know.

SCOT   Depending on how long this takes.

RACHEL   We can play it by ear. Totes chill.

SCOT   The carer's only meant to stay till seven.

RACHEL   Of course. I get that.

SCOT   –
            Rachel I'm forty-seven. You don't want to have
            a chill beer and a burger with me.

RACHEL   Yes I do.

SCOT   Okay so we've stopped with the coy then.

RACHEL   If you don't want to, you can just say.

SCOT   It's not an unappealing prospect.
            But you understand the situation.

RACHEL   Exactly. I understand.

SCOT   I mean you sort of understand.

RACHEL   I understand exactly.

SCOT   But you don't.
            Sweetheart you're twenty-five years old.

RACHEL   –
              Wow.
              Ouch.

SCOT   I don't mean to patronise you.

RACHEL   I'm nearly twenty-six.

SCOT   (*Laughs*.)

RACHEL   Stop it!

SCOT   I'm sorry.

              –

RACHEL   I thought it would just be nice because
              we're in the same sort of situation, you and me.
              And all this stuff we've been doing together to
              Make a fucking difference...
              And I think we get on. Don't we?

SCOT   We're not in the same situation.

RACHEL   Me and my dad.
              You and Carol.

SCOT   I don't want to underplay what you do.

RACHEL   Okay.

SCOT   But our lives are not the same.

RACHEL   I know that no two / situations

SCOT   You go home at the end of the day and you fire
              off a thousand emails and make a vlog about
              a petition and Skype the President.

RACHEL   I've never done that.

SCOT   I've got to clean up my wife's shitty bedsheets.

RACHEL   –

SCOT   Rachel you're fucking fantastic. Please don't
              get me wrong.
              But it's not the same.

Three

JEZ	There's the milk. Bread. Eggs. Beans. There was some veg on reduced-to-clear so I just grabbed a load.
PAULINE	What's this?
JEZ	Dunno but it looks healthy.
PAULINE	What do I do with it?
JEZ	Dunno. Fry it?
PAULINE	– Thanks for all this. Let me get you something.
JEZ	Tenner'll do it. And Mum stuck some brack in. She made it.
PAULINE	Bless her.
JEZ	Said you can freeze it or eat it or whatever. Freezes quite well does brack, actually.
PAULINE	Yeah I remember.
JEZ	Course. It was your mum she got it off of wasn't it? Your mum used to bring it round whenever mine'd had a littl'un. Which was like
PAULINE	All the time
JEZ	Like all the time, yeah, for a while. It's good for the er You know
PAULINE	What?
JEZ	Full of sugar and fruit and that. Good for the you know
PAULINE	?
JEZ	(*Mimes: 'boobs'… 'breast milk'.*)
PAULINE	Yeah I knew that.

JEZ	Not that that's of interest to you.
PAULINE	You never know.
JEZ	– Really?
PAULINE	I mean not *now*. Obviously.
JEZ	Bit old for that aren't you?
PAULINE	Thanks.
JEZ	I don't mean in a bad way.
PAULINE	I don't think there's anything in that could be a good way.
JEZ	Yeah. Sorry.
PAULINE	I'm not quite past it yet you know.
JEZ	Course you're not. Yeah.
	–
JEZ	You heard how Rach is getting on? At her Parliament thing. I saw on Facebook.
PAULINE	Fine. I assume.
JEZ	Have you not seen her posting about it?
PAULINE	I'm not really on Facebook.
JEZ	Yeah you are.
PAULINE	Not really.
JEZ	We're friends. On there.
PAULINE	–
JEZ	Bloody impressive that is, in't it? Good on her. Not quite sure what it's all about you know but Good on her.

PAULINE   It's not actually that complicated.

JEZ   Yeah but I'm thick aren't I.

PAULINE   It's really not all that.

JEZ   Yeah you girls though.

PAULINE   There's this big-shot lawyer helping them it's
            not like she's come up with it on her own.

JEZ   Oh so you've seen then?

PAULINE   I can read the news.

JEZ   She's been on the news?? I'll have to show my
            mum. Can you send the link?
            When's she next home then?

PAULINE   Tomorrow actually.

JEZ   Tomorrow?

PAULINE   I just got a text from her with pick-up demands.

JEZ   Classic Rach.

PAULINE   Do you want to come in?

JEZ   What?

PAULINE   I've got to put this stuff in the fridge.

JEZ   Ummmmmm.
            Er. Yep. Sure. Why not.
            –
            God I've not been in this kitchen in years.
            It's like stepping back in time.

PAULINE   We actually got a new sink.

JEZ   Do you remember when me and Rach nicked
            that bottle of fizz?
            What little shits!

PAULINE   My parents got that for their wedding.
            They always said they were going to have it at
            the christening of their first grandchild.

JEZ   Well at least it didn't go to waste ey?

PAULINE   –

JEZ   Doctor Who ey.
           Back in time!
           But not for you like, nah I guess you're like
           LIVING in the past.
           Like that Victorian school where the kids from
           now have to do the lessons from then. You been
           watching that?

PAULINE   No.

JEZ   You'd like it.

PAULINE   Do you want to stay for dinner?

JEZ   ummmmm
           Er. What you cooking?

PAULINE   This?

JEZ   Yeah I don't really know what that is.

PAULINE   You bought it.

JEZ   Yeah but I don't know if / I'll

PAULINE   It would just be nice to have some company.
           We could watch that Victorian school
           programme.

JEZ   It's on on Tuesdays.

PAULINE   Catch-up?

JEZ   I've seen them all.

PAULINE   Or a film?

JEZ   I dunno Paul no offence or anything but d'you
           not think it'd be a bit weird?

PAULINE   Not really.

JEZ   Kind of like
           hanging out with my mum.

PAULINE   I'm not your mum.

JEZ   Yeah obviously.

PAULINE   I'm not that old.

JEZ   God you didn't take that to heart did you?
Course you're not old I was just having a joke
with you. But like
Just weird, in't it?
Cos we never hung out before.
You were always like
waaaaaaaay above us.

PAULINE   –

You know we're adults now Jez.
We're allowed to form new relationships.

JEZ   Paul I'm really flattered but cards on the table
It would be really weird cos me and your sister
have already had sex.

PAULINE   That's not what I meant.

JEZ   Just wanted to be honest.

PAULINE   When did you have sex??

JEZ   Umm

PAULINE   I don't want to know actually. It's fine.

JEZ   Okay. I'm going to head.
–
I'm sorry Paul. You are cool. Honest. You've
always been like a
Like a fucking statue big-sister woman. All like
huge and marble-y.

PAULINE   What?

JEZ   You're just way out of my league is what I mean.
We can't hang out cos
You're like the Big Sister.
You know?

BIG SISTER.
Biiiiiiiig sister.

–

That's not a comment on your appearance at all.
You're fucking fantastic. We just can't be mates.

Four

PAULINE   Morning.

RACHEL   Shit!
               Sorry.
               You just scared the crap out of me.

PAULINE   –

RACHEL   Didn't know you were up.

PAULINE   It's past eight.

RACHEL   I just thought I'd check on him.
               Thought I could take the morning shift so you
               can have a lie-in.
               It's only just eight.

PAULINE   He's asleep.

RACHEL   Yeah I saw he looks really
               God he looks so small doesn't he.
               Or did you buy bigger pillows?

PAULINE   He's lost weight.

RACHEL   I was making a joke.

PAULINE   It wasn't funny.

RACHEL   Throw me a bone Paul.

               –

PAULINE   He takes his first meds at seven.

RACHEL   Seven. Right.

PAULINE   And it's better if he's eaten something before
               that.

RACHEL   Yeah I know that. I know that drug can be a bit
               / funny on a

PAULINE   So we do breakfast at six-thirty.

RACHEL   Well six-thirty tomorrow, I'm there. Here. I'm
               here.

PAULINE   That'd be great.

RACHEL   That's what I'm here for.

PAULINE   What is?

RACHEL   –
            Was thinking I might go down the surgery
            tomorrow morning.

PAULINE   Why?

RACHEL   Saw the pills on the side. Some of the ones
            they've got him on
            Those are pretty hardcore drugs.

PAULINE   It's a pretty hardcore disease.

RACHEL   There are newer ones though. Better ones.

PAULINE   I'm sure Dr Kelly knows what she's doing.

RACHEL   Of course she does. I'm not saying she doesn't
            I'm just
            like how many patients has she got to look after?
            There's handling the condition and then
            there's like
            Being Proactive.
            There's this really effective new antiemetic.
            It's what they use in America. With the cocktail
            he's on.

PAULINE   Cocktail?

RACHEL   Of drugs.
            Sorry. Shop talk.
            It'll help with the sickness.

PAULINE   I know what an antiemetic does.

RACHEL   It's just I saw the sick bowls by his bed.

PAULINE   It's not that bad every day.

RACHEL   One bad day is enough though. If quality's what
            we're aiming / for

PAULINE   I'd rather you didn't interfere, actually.
            We've spent a really long time getting
            everything sorted at home.

	It's actually been quite a balancing act and Dr Kelly's been really great. She knows what she's doing. She knows Dad.
RACHEL	I'm sure she's wonderful. But everyone's stretched and busy. You know? We need to be more proactive.
PAULINE	Would you please stop saying that.
RACHEL	No I know everyone's doing the best they can. It's just the fucking NHS you know
PAULINE	Rachel, please
RACHEL	No I know the NHS is brilliant. I mean the fucking government.
PAULINE	Do you really have to??
RACHEL	– God does it still really bother you that much?
PAULINE	You're a clever girl I think you can find better ways to express yourself.
RACHEL	You sound just like Dad.
PAULINE	I know you're think you're cool
RACHEL	Oh my God Pauline I do not think that swearing makes me cool. I'm not twelve.
PAULINE	–
RACH	I know someone on that new drug. It's really helping.
PAULINE	Who do you know?
RACHEL	Someone in the campaign group with me.
PAULINE	They're on the drug?
RACHEL	Not him, no.
PAULINE	Him?
RACHEL	Scot. A friend.

PAULINE   A friend?

RACHEL   Yes. I have friends.

PAULINE   You've never mentioned him.

RACHEL   His wife's got it.

PAULINE   His wife?

RACHEL   What is this the copycat game?

PAULINE   –

            Poor man.

RACHEL   Yep.

PAULINE   How bad is she?

RACHEL   Pretty bad.
            She went downhill really quickly.
            Like you know Dad had those five good years
            after we found out when sort of nothing really
            changed.
            For her it was like bam – first symptoms,
            diagnosis, then it was like she just slid down the
            slide all the way to the bottom.
            Fifteen years ago almost to the day. She's like
            textbook.

PAULINE   That must be really hard for him.

RACHEL   Yeah.
            But he's great.
            He's really great with her. And with everyone.
            I have no idea how he does it all he's a superstar.

PAULINE   –

            Careful Rach.

RACHEL   What?

PAULINE   He's a superstar?

RACHEL   He is.

PAULINE   (*Makes a noise.*)

RACHEL   It's platonic.

PAULINE   Is it now.

RACHEL   Yes.

PAULINE   I just know what you're like.
            You enjoy being people's little ray of light.

RACHEL   Well that's very nice of you / but

PAULINE   But then you tend to leave
            and then the sunlight goes
            and then it seems darker than ever.

RACHEL   –

PAULINE   He was at your thing with you Friday?

RACHEL   It wasn't *my* thing

PAULINE   Your government thing

RACHEL   Parliament.

PAULINE   Your thing.

RACHEL   I didn't know you were following.

PAULINE   I've seen the YouTube.

RACHEL   (*Laughs.*)

PAULINE   ?

RACHEL   'The' YouTube.

PAULINE   Just showing an interest in your hobby.

RACHEL   Yeah just a casual attempt to save the lives of
            thousands around the world you know. Just
            chilling.

PAULINE   Thousands?
            One would do.

            –

RACHEL   Look Paul I know you don't really get why I do
            all this

PAULINE   No I get it

RACHEL   It might be too late for Dad but if we get this
patent revoked
that's thousands of people that can have access
to this
fucking
life-changing thing.

PAULINE   Not quite that simple though is it.

RACHEL   It's exactly that simple. It's lives saved.

PAULINE   And then what about all of the other life-saving
drugs? Them ones that haven't been invented
yet?
Who's gonna spend twenty years inventing
those if you're gonna make it so that once
they've been made, anyone can copy them.
I can read the newspapers too Rachel, don't
look so surprised.
I'm not as ignorant as you think.

RACHEL   I've never said you're ignorant. But you just
I just don't think you can quite grasp how
important this is.

PAULINE   How important you are.
I think is what you mean.

RACHEL   –
Anyone can wipe an arse, Pauline.
And you don't have a patent on caring.

Five

PAULINE	Next week. Tuesday of next week. I think. She's going away with her friends first for a little holiday.
SW	That's nice for her.
PAULINE	Some uni friend she's pally with. They're off to his dad's villa or something in the south of France.
SW	Lovely.
PAULINE	And then I've been promised a holiday.
SW	Where d'you think you'll go?
PAULINE	Somewhere by the coast, maybe. Just a train ride away.
SW	Tuesday next is soon though.
PAULINE	Soon?? I don't reckon there's anything *soon* about four years!!
SW	I just thought the end of term would be further off.
PAULINE	Should've been three at most! Sometimes I swear she picked Edinburgh just to spite me!
SW	–
PAULINE	I didn't mean that like that. Please don't write that down.
SW	Why don't you want me to write it down?
PAULINE	I know you're going to read into that.
SW	I write down everything we talk about.
PAULINE	But you're going to use that one to sting me with.
SW	– Pauline. I'm here to support you.

PAULINE	I know.
SW	I'm not here to judge you or to 'sting' you.
PAULINE	I just didn't want you to read more into that comment than it was.
SW	Duly noted. And so what's the plan then, going forwards?
PAULINE	Plan?
SW	Life. When your sister gets home. Have you talked? About sharing? The responsibilities?
PAULINE	I suppose we just make things a lot more equal. I don't think there's any point pretending he's going to get better.
SW	It's important to be practical.
PAULINE	So everything's going to have to get a bit more structure, I think. Say mornings He can still shuffle himself off to the loo and even get his cuppa on a good day but I don't reckon there'll be much more of that left.
SW	So you're aware that somebody will have to be on hand when he wakes up.
PAULINE	For his toilet and such.
SW	Yes.
PAULINE	We could take it in turns.
SW	That sounds sensible.
PAULINE	She's more likely to be out on a Friday or Saturday so I could do weekends.
SW	That's a kind allowance.

PAULINE	Or we could alternate.
SW	And you've spoken about all of this with her?
PAULINE	Yes of course. A bit.
SW	And what are her expectations?
PAULINE	What do you mean expectations?
SW	Does she have a sense of what life looks like as a carer?
PAULINE	None of this is new.
SW	But he is declining.
PAULINE	But she's been around on holidays.
SW	You haven't talked about what it's like full-time?
PAULINE	Look we've always had an understanding. She was always going to come home after university.
SW	What about job prospects?
PAULINE	Sorry?
SW	You have your carer's allowance.
PAULINE	Yeah
SW	And your casual work
PAULINE	I'll be able to do something a bit more part-time though with her around. Maybe some more studying.
SW	Oh?
PAULINE	Why d'you sound so surprised?
SW	I hadn't realised that that was your / plan
PAULINE	I hadn't planned just to look after someone for the rest of my life.

SW	That wasn't what I meant, Pauline.
PAULINE	I was going to work in international development.
SW	Oh?
PAULINE	Oh – yes.
SW	I just haven't ever heard of anyone working in that field before.
PAULINE	What are you writing?
SW	I'm just making notes.
PAULINE	I did an internship. At Oxfam.
SW	Oh?
PAULINE	Stop saying oh!!!

Six

RACHEL	Oh. Fuck. Theo. Fuck fuck fuck I got an email.
THEO	From… you-know-who?
RACHEL	Did you get one??
THEO	– Not yet.
RACHEL	Oh fuck. It's probably a no. They always send out the nos first.
THEO	Not for the final round!
RACHEL	I know it's a no. As if I would get in and you not.
THEO	Open it!!!!
RACHEL	I don't want to.
THEO	Give it here.
RACHEL	No!! I just want to take my time.
THEO	I would literally be gouging my own eyeballs out right now if I was you.
RACHEL	Why?
THEO	How are you not going mental right now?
RACHEL	I just want to live in hope for a bit longer.
THEO	Your answer's right there, you've no hope left.
RACHEL	Not until I've seen it. Until I've read it, I could be living in any number of parallel dimensions that exist after this moment.
THEO	Surely that would be parallel dimensions before the moment?

RACHEL	No after, because all the dimensions are aligned / until
THEO	Open the fucking email Rachel!
RACHEL	(*A deeeeeeeeep breath.*)
THEO	Here. Calm down. Let's just have a lovely little hug. It's alllll going to be ooooooo/kay
RACHEL	THEO YOU BASTARD GIVE IT BACK
THEO	Rach. They're delighted to inform you.
RACHEL	What?
THEO	Delighted.
RACHEL	Seriously?
THEO	They're not pleased. They're fucking delighted.
RACHEL	Oh my God.
THEO	You're in.
RACHEL	Fucking hell.
THEO	'Delighted.'
RACHEL	Check your phone again.
THEO	'Pleased' can go fuck itself. 'Delighted' is what they are. As pie, as cake, as punch, delighted as None of those things are delighted actually are they? Delighted as… Afternoons.
RACHEL	Check your phone!!
THEO	Afternoon delight! It can be our song. What's the time?

	Eleven-forty. Dammit. Oh we'll fudge that moment for the documentary.
RACHEL	What are you going on about??
THEO	The documentary of your life THE MOMENT IT ALL BEGAN. We'll segue into the next scene via the dulcet tones of the Starland Vocal Band.
RACHEL	For fuck's sake just give me your phone to check.
THEO	I didn't get it Rach.
RACHEL	You haven't even looked.
THEO	Found out yesterday.
RACHEL	Why didn't you tell me?
THEO	Didn't want to make you nervous.
RACHEL	Theo
THEO	I'm fine. Honestly. Of course this was the dream but I have loads of other options.
RACHEL	I'm sorry.
THEO	DON'T be sorry. You're smart you're capable you're passionate. You're the bizz.
RACHEL	Stop it.
THEO	You've got that adorable little accent of yours.
RACHEL	What? What d'you mean by that?
	–
RACHEL	You know I don't know if I can even take this.
THEO	Of course you will.
RACHEL	It's fucking London.
THEO	It's all over the world, baby.

RACHEL   The plan was to go home.

THEO   It's New York! Paris! Tokyo!

RACHEL   Is it?

THEO   You're doing the damn grad scheme Rachel.
I'll fucking string you up if you don't.

RACHEL   Don't even know why I went for it.

THEO   Because you wanted it.

RACHEL   Yeah but

THEO   Yeah but yeah but yeah but sherbet lemon.

RACHEL   You're so weird.

THEO   Look what else are you going to do go home
and mop your dying father's brow?

RACHEL   He's not dying.

THEO   Sorry.
Too far.
But seriously Rach, you have to do this. You
know you do. And you'll feel bad and guilty
and blah blah blah but that's all quite boring in
the grand scheme of shit. Things are just
beginning to change here. You're on the
precipice of a new era! Rachel reborn. Leading
the charge. We were the bloody internet
generation and you're not going home now.
Where's the revolution in that?

RACHEL   I suppose I owe it to you.

THEO   You owe me nothing.
I'm just a dinosaur in a young hot bod and not
to sound like a bit of a dick
But you're trendy right now. Someone like
You.
—
You never know how long you're going to be in
vogue right?
I'm not downplaying your actual achievements
here I'm just saying it like it is.

RACHEL   I never would've even applied without you.

THEO   It's fine Rachel. I forgive you.
                And he'll forgive you too. He'll be proud.
                Won't he?

RACHEL   –
                I do want to make him proud.

THEO   How many housemaids does one man need?
                Your sister's already helping out, right?

RACHEL   Don't say it like that.
                She's not a housemaid.
                It's only temporary.

THEO   I just mean, far better for you to head out and
                smash shit so that you can bring home some
                bacon to help them out.

RACHEL   The pay's not exactly brilliant.

THEO   These things never are in the beginning.
                PROSPECTS, Rachel. It's all about the outlook.

RACHEL   Stop it.

THEO   But you know I'm right.

RACHEL   I need to think.

THEO   I think you've already chosen.

Seven

PAULINE   What's that noise?

A song is playing.

It should be a track that you could've listened to on long car journeys: after the puke but before the are-we-nearly-there-yets.

Something that was probably on cassette; which one parent liked more than the other to begin with; but then became such a stalwart family anthem that personal taste went out the window.

RACHEL   You know what it is.

PAULINE   –

RACHEL   (*Moves a little.*
Shoulder shake or shimmy.)

PAULINE   But why is it?

RACHEL   I got a request
From the DJ himself

PAULINE   Dad asked for this??

RACHEL   We've had a great morning.
I went in and I was like HI DAD
and he just beamed at me and went
ahhhhhhhhhh hi mate.

PAULINE   He said that?

RACHEL   Just like he used to.

PAULINE   Just like that?

RACHEL   I nearly started crying.

–

(*Sings along for a line or two.*)

–

PAULINE   You got his lunchtime meds down him?

RACHEL   (*Nods. Sings. Dances.*)

PAULINE   He's not said that to me in months.

RACHEL   What's that?

PAULINE   Hi mate.
             He's not said that.
             He's not said that to me probably since Easter.

RACHEL   (*Sings and dances in a quiet way.*)

PAULINE   Can't believe he said it to you.
             That's good isn't it.
             That that occurred to him again.
             You must of

RACHEL   (*Holds out her hands to her sister,
             still dancing.*)

PAULINE   (*Eventually
             takes one.
             Reluctantly sways.*)

             Why would he say it to you all of a sudden?

RACHEL   (*Shrugs, still singing. Still dancing.*)

PAULINE   (*Still dancing, reluctantly.*)

RACHEL   I dunno Paul.
             Maybe I like jolted it into his memory or
             something.

PAULINE   Little Miss Sunshine.

RACHEL   He didn't say my name.

PAULINE   You remember him calling you that?

RACHEL   I wish you'd not read into everything.

PAULINE   Little Miss Helpful.

RACHEL   He didn't actually call you that. He only said it
             like one time.

Anyway I'd rather be Little Miss Helpful than
Little Miss Sunshine
What good does Little Miss Sunshine do?

PAULINE   She makes him ask for his favourite song.

RACHEL   Oh I basically led him right to that. I was going
on and on about family car journeys and stuff.
I basically practically put it on before he'd even
said it.

PAULINE   Really.

RACHEL   Little Miss Helpful is so the best one to be.
Everyone LOVES Little Miss Helpful.

PAULINE   What and not everyone loves Little Miss
Sunshine?

RACHEL   Oh my God we have stop saying Little Miss
I don't think any human has ever said the words
Little Miss as many times as they have just
been said by us.
Anyway they're proper fucking
reductive, aren't they.

PAULINE   I think they're just children's books.

RACHEL   No but like if you *look* at the characteristics
they give to the misses and the ones they give
to the misters.

PAULINE   Little Miss Bossy?

RACHEL   Exactly.

PAULINE   There's not a Little Mr Bossy.

RACHEL   EXACTLY.

PAULINE   Little Miss Bossy's outgoing and forthright.
Speaks her mind.

RACHEL   Yeah and she's called Little Miss fucking
BOSSY.

PAULINE   I think you're reading too much into this.

RACHEL   (*Laughing.*) I think you're undereducated on
            the politics of semantics.

PAULINE   (*Not laughing.*) Don't be a bitch.

RACHEL   –

PAULINE   –

RACHEL   It's just children's books.

PAULINE   I don't think you're going to change the world
            by getting rid of Little Miss Bossy, or whatever
            it is you're trying to do.

RACHEL   I don't think I ever said I was trying to get rid
            of Little Miss Bossy.

PAULINE   Well good.

RACHEL   Glad that's settled.

PAULINE   You think that you can wear a T-shirt and
            that's it?

RACHEL   What are you on at me for?

PAULINE   You and your slogans.

RACHEL   What's wrong with my T-shirts now?

PAULINE   'My body my rules.' D'you not think it slightly
            defeats the point that it's plastered all over
            your boobs?

RACHEL   IT'S MEANT TO BE PART OF THE POINT.
            (*Still dancing, determinedly – over the
            argument.*)
            Remember this one?
            (*Performs a dance move.*)

PAULINE   (*Stares at her.*)

RACHEL   Remember?
            (*Does it again.*)

PAULINE   Why you doing that?

RACHEL   Go on. Do his bit.

PAULINE   I don't want to.

RACHEL   Go on. I'll do hers. You do his bit.
            (*She does the move again
            waits.*)
            Go on!
            (*She dances again.*)

PAULINE   (*Eventually
            does 'his bit' of the dance.*)

RACHEL   Oh YES! That was amazing.
            God I fucking loved it when Mum and Dad
            did that.
            I thought they were so the coolest.

PAULINE   Why are you here?

RACHEL   What?

PAULINE   Why are you here?
            I'm just a bit confused Rachel because you've
            just turned up
            disrupting his routine and / then

RACHEL   He's not a baby.

PAULINE   Doing Mum's dance moves?
            Why would you do that?
            Why would you bring that up?

RACHEL   –
            It's not like I never come back. I'm here all the
            time.

PAULINE   Scheduled visits. Holidays.

RACHEL   Not fucking scheduled.

PAULINE   Why don't you have a ticket booked back?
            How long are you staying for?
            How come you turned up with just a day's
            notice?
            Are you leaving tonight?
            What about work?

RACHEL   Chill. The fuck. Out. Pauline.
          I'm a grown-up and I can jump on a train
          whenever I like.
          I can call work and come in when I arrange
          with them.
          I'm totally flexible and it's all fine.
          Okay?
          Don't you worry about me.
          I can take care of myself.

Eight

RACHEL   Sorry can you just help me
            Sorry I just don't properly understand.

DOCTOR   I know it all sounds a bit complicated.
            Do you have someone / here…?

RACHEL   It's fine you can just tell me.

DOCTOR   So you know your dad has a bit of atrial
            fibrillation.

RACHEL   He does take his pills. He's really good.

DOCTOR   Do you know what those pills are for?

RACHEL   His heart.

DOCTOR   Sort of. So your dad's heart
            Your heart, my heart, all hearts… are split into
            these chambers.
            How old are you? You've probably done this in
            science.

RACHEL   I'm not great at science.

DOCTOR   Their job is to pump blood around your body.
            Like jsssshhh… jsssshhhh… jsssshhh

RACHEL   I actually don't like science.

DOCTOR   The problem is the chambers in your dad's
            heart can get a bit out of sync. The pills, the
            warfarin, help to keep the blood moving around
            his body.
            It's quite a common problem to have in older
            gentlemen.

RACHEL   My dad's not old.

DOCTOR   Of course not. He's a big strong guy.

RACHEL   He's definitely not a gentleman.

DOCTOR   Maybe we should wait until the rest of your
            family's got here. We can all talk it through
            together.

RACHEL   I'm the one that's here.

DOCTOR	You've done a great job.
RACHEL	I did know that if he's hurt his head you must always go straight to A & E.
DOCTOR	You did exactly the right thing.
RACHEL	I watch a lot of *Helicopter Heroes*.
DOCTOR	Well my apologies we didn't bring the chopper.
RACHEL	He didn't even remember he'd done it. When he fell over.
	Why is that? Why did he go all
DOCTOR	This is where it gets a bit complicated.
RACHEL	it's like he didn't even remember there was even a staircase at all.
	And suddenly he's just on the floor and there was like this horrible
	this horrible crack sound…
	–
DOCTOR	We think that this might have been hiding another problem.
	So you know, it could be a good thing – that your dad's had this fall.
RACHEL	A good thing?
DOCTOR	I know it's hard to understand.
	But baseline is – it's good that we're getting these tests done now.
RACHEL	He's going to be alright?
DOCTOR	He'll recover just fine
	from the fall.
	–
RACHEL	And the other thing? The hidden thing?
DOCTOR	–
RACHEL	Can I go and see him?

DOCTOR	You can soon. But it all looks a bit dramatic at the moment.
RACHEL	When can he come home?
DOCTOR	The specialist doctors want to take a look at those test results before we make any big decisions.
RACHEL	Aren't you a specialist?
DOCTOR	I'm absolutely qualified, don't you worry.
RACHEL	Why does he have to see them then?
DOCTOR	I'm a sort of… specialised generalist.
RACHEL	That sounds made-up.
DOCTOR	Do you have someone else we can call?
RACHEL	I'm trying to get hold of my sister.
DOCTOR	Well if you need anyone to help with that, you get reception / to
RACHEL	She's on holiday. I'm getting this funny noise in the phone, here listen – I've never heard it ring like that. She's normally the one that She's a lot older than me. I was an accident so I'm a lot younger. Not an accident they always said a happy surprise. But she's the one that would normally I'm doing my GCSEs. I've got maths tomorrow.
DOCTOR	Why don't you come over here to the nurses' station. You know, the nurses on this ward have the best-stocked biscuit tin in the entire hospital. You just can't let anyone else know, or they'll be queuing up.
RACHEL	I think I just need to talk to my sister.

Nine

LOUIE	Soooooooooooo ?
PAULINE	–
LOUIE	Is this a happy silence or a – Paul I'd appreciate something. Flicker of an eyebrow or
PAULINE	I had no idea.
LOUIE	No? We're in Tenerife.
PAULINE	On holiday.
LOUIE	Bit of a special holiday though right?
PAULINE	It's been lovely. I've loved it.
LOUIE	Be more specific.
PAULINE	I mean I love the holiday and I love Tenerife and we've been having such a lovely time and it's been so nice to get away from everything at home.
LOUIE	Okay.
PAULINE	I just actually haven't thought about You got a ring and everything.
LOUIE	I dropped all the appropriate hints.
PAULINE	Yeah?
LOUIE	I asked for your ring size.
PAULINE	Yeah you did.
LOUIE	We've talked about getting married.
PAULINE	We've talked about having kids!
LOUIE	Yes…

PAULINE	In a faraway sort of way.
LOUIE	I dunno maybe it felt more faraway to you. Do you not think it's time? A lot of other people are.
PAULINE	Yeah I know. I don't know why I'm so
LOUIE	I thought we needed something to I don't like being so far away from you.
PAULINE	I'm sorry.
LOUIE	I don't want you to apologise I want us to do something about it.
PAULINE	I know, I'm / sorry
LOUIE	Paul – stop apologising! You've had stuff you had to be around for.
PAULINE	There's stuff I wanted to do.
LOUIE	I know. Your dad, your sister. You're brilliant at looking after everyone. After everything with / your
PAULINE	No I mean now. I think that's why I hadn't like… thought about it. I think. I still want to do my MA.
LOUIE	Okay.
PAULINE	I do want to move out.
LOUIE	Exactly.
PAULINE	I just thought I might have more time.
LOUIE	When?
PAULINE	Sort of between this last bit and this bit you're talking about.
LOUIE	?

PAULINE   Like it was meant to be five years, five years,
            five years.
            I'll do my MA get myself set up – five years.
            I'll focus on my career – smash it. Five years.
            I'll get married and
            you know, the rest.
            Five years.

LOUIE   And where are we now?

PAULINE   Delayed.

LOUIE   And where does that leave me then?

PAULINE   Hanging out in duty-free?

LOUIE   Paul

PAULINE   I'm sorry. I'm know this is
            For you
            Like you got the ring and everything.
            I just thought I had more time.

LOUIE   Time to do what?

PAULINE   I dunno. Stuff. The stuff I wanted to do before
            everything else.

LOUIE   What? Other people?
            Other guys?

PAULINE   That's not what I mean.

LOUIE   Then I don't get it.

PAULINE   Just
            stuff I want to
            achieve.

LOUIE   So achieve it.

PAULINE   On my own.

LOUIE   Right.

PAULINE   I don't want us to break up!!

LOUIE   I'm really struggling to understand how that
            doesn't mean you want to break up.

PAULINE	I don't really know how to make it make sense out loud.
LOUIE	So let's get married.
PAULINE	–
LOUIE	I don't want to be the dick who says he's been patient.
PAULINE	You have been.
LOUIE	You're so busy giving yourself to other people all the time
PAULINE	That's not fair.
LOUIE	No?
PAULINE	It's just been necessary to It's not like I've put anyone Chosen to put other people
LOUIE	But you have. And you do.
PAULINE	They needed me.
LOUIE	I need you.
PAULINE	Who else was gonna look after them?
LOUIE	They're adults.
PAULINE	Rach is hardly an adult.
LOUIE	(*A noise.*)
PAULINE	What?
LOUIE	Nothing.
PAULINE	No go on.
LOUIE	You'll just get angry.
PAULINE	I won't get angry.
LOUIE	Yeah right.
PAULINE	–

LOUIE   It's just you've said it yourself Paul.
          She has to be the centre of attention, that girl.
          And as soon as she's not she kicks off. And you
          and your dad, you let her get away with murder
          cos she's the baby of the family.
          And she's just not. Any more.
          Think about all the stuff that you were doing at
          her age.

PAULINE   She's still a kid.

LOUIE   She is not a kid.
          Certainly doesn't look like a kid.

PAULINE   Jesus Louie.

LOUIE   What about your graduation dinner? With that
          whole bloody drama of hers. She barely made it
          through the dough balls.

PAULINE   Yeah.
          I know.
          But that's not quite fair. It's been hard / for her

LOUIE   See I knew exactly this would happen.
          As soon as I try to have an opinion on the
          wunderkind.

PAULINE   I'm not saying you're / not right

LOUIE   I'm just saying exactly what you always cry
          about to me.
          She's always gotta be the centre of the universe
          blah blah
          Everyone loves Rachel and no one loves me
          And I just have to sit there and listen to it but
          like
          God forbid I say anything.

PAULINE   It's just
          she's my sister.

LOUIE   So you're allowed to say it.
          And I'm just not.

PAULINE   I think that's probably it.

            –

LOUIE   Fuck me. Here I am asking you to marry me
            And we're talking about your family. Again.

            –

            Your phone's ringing.

PAULINE   I'll get it later.

LOUIE   Who is it?

PAULINE   It's nothing.
            It's Rachel. I'll call her back.

LOUIE   Go on answer, I know you want to.

PAULINE   –
            You shouldn't make me choose.
            It's not fair.

LOUIE   I think you've already chosen.

Ten

RACHEL   Did he just
              ?

              –

              You heard that
              Right?

              –

PAULINE   He's just confused.

              –

              Stop touching your face like that.   → Patronising
                                                          like a mum
              –

              Stop it!

              –

RACHEL   I think I might
              be sick.

PAULINE   Don't be oversensitive.

RACHEL   I'm not being oversensitive he just acted like I /
              was

PAULINE   He's just confused.

RACHEL   I fucking hate it when you call me that.

PAULINE   It's not an insult

RACHEL   Sounds like an insult.

PAULINE   It's a descriptive word.

RACHEL   Feels like an insult.

              –   → Sarcastic

PAULINE   Feeling better?

RACHEL   I wasn't actually going to be sick. Obviously.

              –

RACHEL   Do you think he actually thought
            that I was her?

PAULINE   No.   → *reassuring*

RACHEL   Everyone always used to say though.
            You like him and me like her.
            Like they managed to split themselves in half
            instead of sharing.   → *quizzical* .

PAULINE   I don't see it. I've never seen it.
            Your hair's a different colour.

RACHEL   She used to dye it.

PAULINE   –

RACHEL   I don't mind.

PAULINE   What?

RACHEL   I thought she was pretty.

PAULINE   Everyone thinks their mum's pretty when
            they're a kid.   ← *joking*

RACHEL   You didn't?
            Gee thanks.

PAULINE   I said everyone didn't I.

            –

RACHEL   Has he ever done that before?

PAULINE   I've never heard him say her name.

RACHEL   What, never?

PAULINE   Obviously before.

RACHEL   But not since?

            –

            Let's have a drink.
            This is too weird.
            You on red? I bought this.
            Was on offer at the Waitrose in King's Cross.

PAULINE   Waitrose? → *mocking*

RACHEL   Shiraz I think.

PAULINE   Very nice.

RACHEL   I like a New Zealand.

PAULINE   I wouldn't know.

RACHEL   Corkscrew?

PAULINE   I wouldn't know a New Zealand wine if it bit me in the arse.

RACHEL   I mean quite why a New Zealand wine would be biting you in the arse

PAULINE   Second drawer down.
Not that second drawer. The other second drawer.

RACHEL   Why d'you keep them in here now?

PAULINE   They've always been in there.

RACHEL   They've not.

PAULINE   They have. | *builds up*

RACHEL   They used to be

PAULINE   They were always in there.

RACHEL   No they weren't.   ← *irritated*

PAULINE   Yes. They were.
            –   ← *sit down*

            Thanks for the wine.

RACHEL   My pleasure.

PAULINE   Here's to you.

RACHEL   Me?

PAULINE   Homecoming.

RACHEL   Alright.

PAULINE   Prodigal daughter returns.   ← *joking / resentful*

            –

RACHEL   Top-up?

PAULINE   I haven't finished…
            Alright then.

            –

            You're right you know.   *sentimental*
            You do look like her.

RACHEL   I know.

PAULINE   Your eyes are like hers.
            Your chin.

RACHEL   My chin?

PAULINE   Your pointy chin.

RACHEL   My chin is not pointy.

PAULINE   Angled.
            Sharp.
            In a good way. Obviously.
            That little model sharp-cut chin of yours.

            –

RACHEL   I didn't know about my chin.

PAULINE   Did you not.

RACHEL   Do we have a photo?

PAULINE   Why d'you want a photo?

RACHEL   I've not seen any photos in years.

PAULINE   Sorry no can do.

RACHEL   Maybe in the attic?

PAULINE   He burned them.   ← *serious but fast*

RACHEL   What? The photos
            All of the photos?

PAULINE   All of them.

RACHEL   Even the ones with
            With like us in them?
            Even like all of our family photos?

PAULINE   He was that bloke.

RACHEL   I never knew that.

PAULINE   We had a big old bonfire.   *lighthearted*
            Just out there.

RACHEL   How come I never knew that?

PAULINE   I thought it might upset you.

RACHEL   You really should've told me about that.

PAULINE   It upset me.   *sad*

RACHEL   Yeah but

PAULINE   It was brutal.   *← sad*
            Might as well have had a Guy Fawkes of her
            on top.   *jokey*
            A Mum Fawkes.
            Ha.

RACHEL   I should have known about that.

PAULINE   Well I apologise
            Rachel
harsh   For not telling you about the bonfire that Dad
            and I had together
            When we burned all the photos of our mother.

            —

RACHEL   Can I top you up?

PAULINE   Go for it.

            —

RACHEL   Paul? Glass?

PAULINE   Are you having more?

RACHEL   Yeah.

PAULINE	Well none for me then thanks.
RACHEL	There's plenty left.
PAULINE	All the more for you.
RACHEL	What the fuck just give me your glass.
PAULINE	I'll suppose I'll be doing the morning shift.
RACHEL	What?
PAULINE	Sorry – had you not thought about the hangover?
RACHEL	It's two glasses
PAULINE	Two glasses sends me a little bit funny these days. Must be because I don't get to drink an awful lot.
RACHEL	Have you got a problem with me drinking now?
PAULINE	I don't have a problem with you drinking.
RACHEL	Cos it seems like you have a problem with me drinking.
PAULINE	No it's fine. Here. Let me get you another.
RACHEL	– You know, being miserable is not an achievement Pauline. It's not like a badge of honour. And taking care of yourself. Treating yourself nicely That doesn't make me bad person either.
PAULINE	I suppose I'm too busy taking care of other people to take care of myself.
RACHEL	Maybe you'd have a friend to have a drink with if you did. *Beat.* Someone other than me.
PAULINE	You?

RACHEL   Yeah the girl who came to visit you and bought the bottle of wine.

PAULINE   We're not friends. We're sisters.

RACHEL   Yeah. Sorry. I forgot we can't be both.

PAULINE   –

What's with the showcase Rachel?
I'm your only audience left can we not just talk straight please?
No need for the drawn-out performance.

RACHEL   You have such a low opinion of me.

PAULINE   I just know you too well.

RACHEL   Or hardly at all.

PAULINE   Or just like – all your life.

RACHEL   –

I wanted us to sit down and have a proper grown-up chat about this but
You know since you're pretty much determined to make out like I'm
I dunno
Some sort of villain that's come back to haunt you.
You're right. I might as well just tell you.
–

I've decided I'm going to find Mum.

Eleven

JEZ	(*Crashing in*.) Shhhhhhhhhhh!!!!
RACHEL	SHHHHHHHHHHHHHHHH.
JEZ	Shush.
RACHEL	Huuuuusssssshhhhh.
JEZ	hahahahahahahah.
RACHEL	– I don't even know if anyone's even in.
JEZ	Where else'd they bed?
RACHEL	(*Laughs*.)
JEZ	Be. They should in bed. Where else WOULD they bed? Be. Haha.
RACHEL	You're fucking drunk.
JEZ	You're fucking drunk.
RACHEL	I'm more drunk than you are.
JEZ	Yes.
RACHEL	No you are more drunk. And if I am as drunk as you are then I'm allowed to be cos we were equally and I'm a lot smaller.
JEZ	You're tiny.
RACHEL	Not that small.
JEZ	I could pick you up.
RACHEL	Don't. You. Dare. Jeremy Long.
	JEZ *picks her up*.
	JEZ *holds her*.
	…*puts her down*.
	Let's find more booze.

JEZ   What they got?

RACHEL   I
                  Fucking
                  HATE
                  red wine.

JEZ   Who the fuck drinks red wine??

RACHEL   Why would they not have any cider????

JEZ   Bet *Pauline* drinks red wine.

RACHEL   Hang on. There's something

JEZ   *Pauline's* so fancy since she went to uni.

RACHEL   I'm going to go to uni.

JEZ   One red wine sir IF YOU PLEASE for HER!

RACHEL   I promise you
                  I swear down
                  On my fucking
                  Life
                  On my dad's life
                  I will never drink red wine.

JEZ   Gives you a black mouth.

RACHEL   Exactly.

JEZ   No one wants to kiss anyone with a black mouth.

RACHEL   Found this.

JEZ   What's THAT?

RACHEL   THIS is CHAMPAGNE. I think.

JEZ   Seriously?

RACHEL   Open it.

JEZ   No way!

RACHEL   Go on open it.

JEZ   I'm not opening your folks' Champagne Rach.
                  You're mad.

RACHEL   Who gives a fuck.

JEZ   Jesus you're proper smashed you are.

RACHEL   They got this on their wedding day.

JEZ   Serious??

RACHEL   And they're always saaaaaving it for a special
            occasion.

JEZ   Christmas?

RACHEL   She said she was going to open it at the birth of
            her first grandchild.
            HA.

JEZ   Rach!

RACHEL   (*Pops the cork.*)
            As if *she's* getting invited to that.
            (*Downs a good quarter of the bottle
            – and probably burps.*)

            Here.

JEZ   Your dad might've wanted to save that.

RACHEL   For a special occasion??
            Tell you what.
            I'm never waiting for a special occasion. Not
            for the rest of my whole life.

JEZ   You gonna get sad drunk are you now?

RACHEL   No.
            Course not.
            She doesn't want to be my mum?
            Gives a fuck. You know?

JEZ   If you're gonna cry we should call you up
            a girlfriend.

RACHEL   You're such a prick.

JEZ   Not a boy-friend.

RACHEL   You're not my boyfriend.

JEZ   Never said I was your boyfriend.
                  Boy.
                  Friend.

RACHEL   Yeah.

JEZ   You're obsessed you are.

RACHEL   Am not.

JEZ   With me.

RACHEL   AM NOT.

JEZ   As if you'd say no.

RACHEL   As if *you'd* say no.

JEZ   Yeah probably not

                  Some kissing and stumbling.

RACHEL   Not in there.

JEZ   Why not?

RACHEL   Paul's in there.

JEZ   Why's Paul sleeping in your room? What's
                  wrong with hers?

RACHEL   –

JEZ   Oh shit is that where your mum??

RACHEL   Shut up

JEZ   Fuck she did it IN THE HOUSE?
                  She did it IN HER DAUGHTER'S ROOM?
                  Every time??

RACHEL   Let's go back to yours.

JEZ   That is low.
                  How d'you know she didn't do it in yours?
                  How d'you know she didn't do it here?
                  Or here?
                  Or here?

RACHEL	Shut the fuck up Jez. It's not funny.
	That's where she was sleeping. In Paul's.
	Since like last Christmas.
JEZ	Sleeping or…
	…
RACHEL	Thought you didn't want to talk about it?
JEZ	Don't want you to *cry* about it. I don't mind talking about it.
RACHEL	Well
	she's a bitch
	has been for months so
	that's that.
JEZ	Come on Rach.
RACHEL	What?
JEZ	Your mum's not a bitch.
RACHEL	What do you know about it?
JEZ	You shouldn't say stuff like that.
RACHEL	Why not it's true. She's fucking selfish.
JEZ	She might come back.
RACHEL	Don't want her to.
JEZ	Can't imagine my mum going off.
RACHEL	She never would.
JEZ	We'd all like
	die.
RACHEL	It's like we're all just walking around a field we think's a field but it's actually a volcano, is how it feels.

Twelve

PAULINE   Because it's like there's this massive empty
             hole under us and

LOUIE   Who's gonna?

             PAULINE *and* RACHEL *stand right on the*
             mouth of the volcano.

             What?

             Magma rising.

             Paul?

             Earth shaking.

Eleven / Twelve

RACHEL/
PAULINE   Because it feels

PAULINE   feels like there's this massive

RACHEL   It feels to me like there's this massive

PAULINE   massive empty hole

RACHEL   Like there's this massive empty hole under me.

             The sounds of the eruption cease.

             And I don't know how to fill / it.

PAULINE   and I don't know how I'm gonna fill it.

Thirteen

RACHEL	Are you going to say something?
PAULINE	I should probably check on Dad.
RACHEL	Paul
PAULINE	Rachel?
RACHEL	Dad's fine.
PAULINE	Didn't realise you were telepathic now too.
RACHEL	Smart.
PAULINE	What d'you mean 'find'? What you talking about 'find'???? You can't find someone that's not lost. She didn't wander off the trail in the rainforest. She's not a missing person in a conflict zone.
RACHEL	No I know that. But I think we should talk about this.
PAULINE	Why?
RACHEL	I think we just should.
PAULINE	I don't think we need to.
RACHEL	Well I want to.
PAULINE	Well then.
	–
RACHEL	That's not an unreasonable thing to say. I'm not Demanding to get my own way here. I'm actually being very adult about this situation.
PAULINE	I don't think you'll ever be an adult Rachel. You don't have it in you.
RACHEL	What does that even mean???
PAULINE	Being an adult's not just about how many years you're totting up. You can't tally it in your notebook and then give yourself a tick.

RACHEL   I am twenty-five years old.

PAULINE   You're a child.
            And you always will be.
            Because you have never had to think about
            another human being.
            It's always been The Rachel Show hasn't it.
            It's always going to be The Rachel Show and
            d'you know what?
            I didn't mind. For ages. I didn't mind.
            Cos actually you were quite fun.
            You've always been sparky and
            Loveable.
            But I was clever.
            And I was
            Diligent.
            And you just had to take that too because
            You just had to be the centre of the universe the
            sunshine
            you couldn't let me
            You never let me have a single thing.

RACHEL   What the hell are you talking about?!
            You literally came first! You have no idea what
            it's like to be someone's sister.

PAULINE   You have no idea what it's like to be YOUR
            sister.

RACHEL   I try so hard to be nice to you. You don't
            understand how fucking hard you make it,
            you're a fucking misery to be around!

PAULINE   Not everybody's life can be a delightful little
            hop and skip around / the city

RACHEL   Oh fuck off do I hop and / skip

PAULINE   Not everybody can be Little Miss / Sunshine

RACH   I swear to God Pauline.
            If you call me that one more time…
            You're spiteful. That's what you are.
            You don't have any interest in being okay or
            being happy

You're too proud of being put upon and d'you
know what?
It's outdated, that is. People are bored of people
claiming that misery makes you better. It doesn't.
It just makes you miserable.
And now –
You're just a spiteful woman.

–

PAULINE   Take that back.

RACHEL   I want to be happy.

PAULINE   And what have you got to be sad about? Go on.
Tell me how hard your life is.

RACHEL   Can you for one second just listen to me
without actually just thinking about yourself?
Think about me
For a moment
Like I'm a different country.
Even better – we're continents.
Imagine that we're fucking continents on
opposite sides of the world.
No borders shared. Not even an ocean.
As far apart as you can get.
Just –
Keep that image in your head, for just a minute.
Because I actually came back here, this
weekend, out of respect for you.
I wanted us to have a conversation before I

–

You know what. Fine.
I lied before. I did.
I'm not planning on getting in touch with Mum.
I've already done it.
And she wants to come and say goodbye to Dad.

Fourteen

PROFESSOR   It's an interesting background to approach from.

PAULINE   Really?

PROFESSOR   Not usual.

PAULINE   I think that actually
              the combination with literature
              I think there's loads that I can bring from
              having trained my brain in that kind of analysis.

PROFESSOR   I wasn't talking about your bachelor's.

PAULINE   Oh?

PROFESSOR   I meant your *background* background.
              This gap…

PAULINE   I did an internship with Oxfam.

PROFESSOR   And worked on a strawberry farm.

PAULINE   Oh um
              Yeah. I mean that's not strictly relevant.
              I've been saving up.
              The strawberries were just during the summer.
              Obviously.
              Sorry I only put it down because I had this
              mentor
              I won this bit of mentoring, and he said not to
              leave any gaps on my CV.
              I know it's not very relevant / but

PROFESSOR   Au contraire!
              What did you learn from the strawberries?

PAULINE   From
              ?

PROFESSOR   The strawberries. Yes.

PAULINE   –

PROFESSOR   I'm fascinated.

PAULINE   I'm sorry I don't understand.

PROFESSOR   Tell me something I don't know, Pauline.
             Tell me about the *strawberries*.

PAULINE   It was just a summer job.
             I was a picker at the beginning of the season
             and then they also do
             …Pick Your Own?

PROFESSOR   (*Shakes his head vigorously.*
             Nods his head encouragingly.)

PAULINE   And then I would
             be on the till in the farm shop.

             –

             At Oxfam I spent two / months

PROFESSOR   I've already heard about Oxfam today.

             What I'm looking for, Pauline
             is Lateral Thinking.
             Do you know what I mean by that?

PAULINE   I know what lateral means.

PROFESSOR   We're in the business of changing the world.

PAULINE   That's why I applied / to

PROFESSOR   Do you know what's happening at the moment?

PAULINE   Um

PROFESSOR   Banks collapsing. Communities crumbling.
             Economies crashing.

PAULINE   Yes I know.

PROFESSOR   Greece!

PAULINE   Greece.

PROFESSOR   Challenging times ahead.

PAULINE   Yes. Which is why I really want to make a /
             difference

PROFESSOR   (*Sighs.*)
             My apologies.
             I'm just slightly disappointed.

PAULINE   Oh.

PROFESSOR   You see *on paper* I got *quite excited* about
              meeting you.
              It's really rather rare to get someone from *your*
              sort of background with the *ambition* of
              progressing into the *high heights* of higher
              education in this *particular* area. We're mostly
              a bunch of stodges. Passing the stodge on and
              on. You see?

PAULINE   The stodge?

PROFESSOR   The noose of funding is closing ever tighter
              around my neck.
              My hands are tied.
              We'll have to accept more from China or
              America. Gotta have that dollar dollar.
              Or that yuan yuan, should I say.

PAULINE   What did I do wrong?

PROFESSOR   That was a joke.

PAULINE   (*Laughs?*)

PROFESSOR   I wasn't being racist.

PAULINE   I didn't / think

PROFESSOR   The strawberries, Pauline!
              You should have elucidated on the
              STRAWBERRIES!

PAULINE   What do you want to know about the
              strawberries??

PROFESSOR   The strawberries as *metaphor*.
              We could have learned so much more from the
              strawberry farm than three months filling in
              spreadsheets for Oxfam.

PAULINE   No I totally see that.
              I personally completely understand how my
              work in the farm shop and at the swimming
              baths and basically practically having to raise
              my little sister

How all of that is so much more relevant to
international development / cos

PROFESSOR   You were a swimming instructor?
How singular!

PAULINE   –
I just didn't think that all of that is what you'd
want to hear from me cos
Everything that I've read on the internet, and
what my teachers told me, and what that
mentor said
Was to stick to the curriculum.
To get my grades. Buy my suit from Next.
Say exactly what you want to hear.

PROFESSOR   Such an unfortunately common misconception.
There's nothing we should like to hear more
than something other than what you might think
we want to hear.

PAULINE   Well.
Thank you for taking the time.
I'll try and take your feedback on board. Maybe
next year.

PROFESSOR   Next year?
Oh no no no no no no no no you
misunderstand me.
No you were always getting a place Pauline.
No fear of that!

PAULINE   Really?

PROFESSOR   No no no no no this was more of a formality
really.
Your marks are quite spectacular. And your
written work is reasonably exceptional.

PAULINE   Oh my God.
Thank you!

PROFESSOR   And we do have those quotas to fill.
You're a bit of a gift really!
We'll have to get you on the soundbites.

Fifteen

RACHEL	She's lying sir!!
TEACHER	Rachel how many times do we have to have this conversation?
RACHEL	But sir I never!
TEACHER	I'm getting so bored of this.
RACHEL	Me too.
TEACHER	Hey. I will put you in detention.
RACHEL	You can't sir I've got to get my sister after school.
TEACHER	What you're in charge of pick-ups now?
RACHEL	No! Mum's getting me and then we're going on to get Paul cos she's getting the train cos she's in London for the day and if Mum doesn't get me first then she'll have to go all the way back round again and then she'll go mental.
TEACHER	Or you can get the bus.
RACHEL	– Sir don't make me get the bus.
TEACHER	Can we have a proper conversation please Rachel?
RACHEL	I am talking.
TEACHER	No a conversation. I would like you to listen as well as speak. To talk in response to the things that I am saying to you.
RACHEL	Well you need to listen to me as well then.
TEACHER	(*Sigh*.) Throw me a bone here Rachel. What's going on?
RACHEL	(*Shrugs*.)
TEACHER	You know your behaviour's getting worse.
RACHEL	(*Nods*.)

TEACHER	And you know that it didn't used to be like this. We used to get on. Didn't we.
RACHEL	(*Sniffs*.)
TEACHER	Would you like a tissue?
RACHEL	(*Shakes her head*.) Yeah.
TEACHER	Your work's good Rachel. Why the attitude?
RACHEL	(*Shrugs*.)
TEACHER	Now comes the talking bit.
RACHEL	I dunno.
TEACHER	You dunno?
RACHEL	It's just really hard.
TEACHER	What is?
RACHEL	Being a girl.
TEACHER	I know it can feel really hard being a teenager.
RACHEL	No you don't know sir.
TEACHER	– Yeah okay maybe I don't know. Is there something specific going on? Maybe you can have a chat with one of the female teachers.
RACHEL	(*Shakes her head*.) They're all stupid sir.
TEACHER	Hey. No thank you. – What about your sister?
RACHEL	–
TEACHER	D'you talk to her?
RACHEL	(*Shrugs*.)
TEACHER	I remember Pauline. How's she doing?

RACHEL	(*Shrugs*.)
TEACHER	I taught her too. Didn't have any of this trouble I must say.
RACHEL	That's cos Pauline's fucking perfect.
TEACHER	Hey! I'll pretend I didn't hear that. – I'm sure she's not perfect. None of us are perfect.
RACHEL	Yeah she is. She always does everything right.
TEACHER	Like what?
RACHEL	Dad calls her Mary Poppins.
TEACHER	(*Laughs*.) Do you want to be Mary Poppins?
RACHEL	As if.
TEACHER	Pauline went on to uni didn't she? Good on her. She back home now?
RACHEL	(*Nods*.)
TEACHER	Quite an age gap between the two of you isn't there.
RACHEL	Nine or ten depending on the month.
TEACHER	How long's she been back?
RACHEL	Like a year. Saving for her master's.
TEACHER	Wow. Well done her.
RACHEL	–
TEACHER	House feeling a little crowded these days?
RACHEL	(*Shrugs*.)
TEACHER	Don't worry Rachel. You'll get there.
RACHEL	Get where?
TEACHER	Uni. Grown up. Whatever you want to do.

RACHEL   I don't wanna go uni.

TEACHER   No?

RACHEL   I wanna do my own thing.

TEACHER   A lot more people go to university than just
            your sister you know.

RACHEL   Yeah I know but she was the first so it's like
            her thing.

TEACHER   –
            I know it can feel
            Well, I don't know exactly, obviously. What's
            going on in your own head.
            But I know that it took me a long time to find
            out exactly what was special about me. And it
            was really frustrating for a long time. Waiting
            to know what *my thing* was.
            I've got three brothers.

RACHEL   Four of you??

TEACHER   I have a sneaky suspicion my mum was holding
            out for a girl.

RACHEL   Least she was holding out for something.
            Least you wasn't just an accident after the
            perfect hole-in-one.

TEACHER   –
            That's a disgusting metaphor.

RACHEL   (*Tries not to giggle.*)

TEACHER   Fourteen's tough.
            –
            You want to know what I think of you so far
            though?

RACHEL   Attitude problem?

TEACHER   Well yes there's that.
            But no. I was going to say
            I think you're very funny.
            I think you're very bright.

I think you're quite stubborn, and sometimes
you like to do stuff just because people think
you won't.
I think you're sensitive. And I think you're very
generous.

RACHEL   –
                (*Sniffs.*)
                Alright sir what d'you fancy me or something?

TEACHER   (*Sigh.*)
                Get out of my classroom Rachel.

Sixteen

PAULINE   Get out.

RACHEL   You can't tell me / to get out!

PAULINE   I think you should leave.

RACHEL   You can't tell me to leave.
             This is just as much my house as it is yours.

PAULINE   You don't live here any more.

RACHEL   Legally – it's just as much mine.

PAULINE   –

RACHEL   Sorry did you not think I was enough of an
             adult to be aware of our legal situation?
             He's had conversations with me, too, Pauline.
             I'm well aware of what we're both entitled to.

             –

             I'm not the villain here.

PAULINE   But you're siding with her.

RACHEL   There's not sides any more.

PAULINE   Yes there are.

RACHEL   He doesn't even remember it.
             How can there be sides when one person can't
             even remember what it is that the other did to
             hurt them?

PAULINE   I remember.

RACHEL   She didn't do it to us.

PAULINE   Yes she did.

RACHEL   She didn't *mean* to.

PAULINE   There's no such thing
             as not *meaning* to
             when you're a mother.

RACHEL   Bullshit. Just
             bullshit!!

We're all just human at the end of the day and
–

Like I get that she fucked up back then but
I was really young, actually. To lose her.
To lose that person from my life. The woman
who should've…

PAULINE   The woman who should've been there.
            The woman who should
            be here.

            –

            That's what she signed up for.

RACHEL   That's what I mean though.
            I mean it's not contract law.
            It's sex followed by a collection of cells.
            It's the easiest fucking thing in the world
            I could head out right here right now and come
            back in ten minutes and have 'signed up' for it.

PAULINE   Pop round Jez's?

RACHEL   –
            What the fuck was *that*?

PAULINE   Nothing.

RACHEL   Are you
            jealous
            of Jez??

PAULINE   Of course I'm not jealous of Jez.

RACHEL   Cos he's fucking stupid.

PAULINE   I know that.

RACHEL   And really just normal looking.

PAULINE   I never said I wanted to sleep with Jez.

RACHEL   And I'll be brutally honest
            has a below-average-sized

PAULINE   Give the lad a break he was like sixteen
            years old.

RACHEL   I'm not sure that's the sort of thing that gets
           better with age Paul.

           –

RACHEL   You had the bonfire.
           You got to decide.
           And I was fifteen years old and I didn't have
           anyone.

PAULINE   Yeah I guess
           I suppose you probably needed her when
           When you needed coaching through your maths
           GCSE, when you were about to fail it for the
           third time or
           You probably needed her to pick you up from
           all those parties?
           When you were being sick? On God-knows-
           what.
           You probably needed her that time when you
           got your period and it was so bad you needed
           hot-water bottles holding to your stomach when
           you were sitting on the loo.
           You needed someone like her to literally wipe
           the blood from your thigh
           And from where it'd dripped on the floor.
           Someone who'd never mention it to anyone.
           Someone who'd just sit there and do it for you.
           Holding the bog roll.

RACHEL   I never asked you for any of that stuff.

PAULINE   And I suppose it's too much to get a thank-you.

RACHEL   Why should I have to thank you for stuff I never
           asked for??

PAULINE   You just take take take / take take

RACHEL   Oh and I guess you think you're just all give
           give / fucking give

PAULINE   This isn't about me.

RACHEL   OF COURSE IT'S ABOUT YOU.

PAULINE   It's about her.

RACHEL   It is about US.
            I'm here Paul. I'm standing right here.
            I came back for this.
            I didn't have to do that.

PAULINE   You did.

RACHEL   No, I didn't.

PAULINE   You did.
            You did have to come back for this Rachel.
            You did.
            You said you would. That was the deal.
            You promised.
            And actually you know I think back in my head
            and maybe
            You know maybe you didn't promise.
            I mean it feels like, at some point, there was
            a conversation in which you got down on one
            knee and held out your sword to me
            And said – I promise.
            I'll come back and take my turn.
            But obviously that didn't happen. Like that.
            But there's something you're missing.
            And I agree with you.
            That certain things shouldn't necessarily fall on
            certain people. It isn't fair.
            But they do.
            That's life.
            And being a daughter means

            –

            Don't shake your head at me.

            –

            Do you remember the last time I went on
            holiday. When you came and took care of Dad.
            And I went to Skegness.

RACHEL   Of all the fucking places.

PAULINE   I liked Skegness.
            I like the train ride and the chips so what?
            I didn't have time to learn how to say hi and
            thanks and half a pint please.
            –
            I liked walking on the beach in the morning.
            In the habit of rising early
            And so I'd find myself awake at six and it'd be
            quiet but for the bin men
            and breakfast didn't start till seven. But this one
            morning I woke up even earlier. Just tossing
            and turning. And no point in lying there wasting
            the day
            so I get myself up
            go out down to the beach.
            And there is this giant on it.
            I thought it must have been a shipwreck at first.
            But then I notice it moving.
            Heaving
            This giant, heaving thing, in the dark.
            But when I go down to the sand
            It's a whale.
            Bigger than
            Anything I have ever seen.
            Taller than me. Could fit at least fifty of me
            alongside that thing, my neck, I have to crane
            up to see
            and it is still
            Breathing.
            Huge
            Heaving breaths.
            I lay my hand on it.
            I think it felt me there with it.
            And I just thought
            I would want to know I'm not alone, at a time
            like that.
            I stand there with my hands on it and then the
            sun starts coming up and I notice behind it
            I hadn't even seen before but just twenty metres
            or so behind

There's another one. And then another next
to that.
And then I see in the water this shape and
there's another one coming too, close now,
close to beaching itself too
So I splash in and I'm shouting
As if that's gonna making any difference
GET BACK GET BACK GET BACK YOU
STUPID THING SAVE YOURSELF
In the sea up to my knees like a madwoman
trying to push against this hundred-tonne thing.
And crying. And screaming.
As if any good that was gonna do. My weight.
Against all of that.

–

Four of them stranded on the beach.
Sperm whales, they said.

RACHEL   I remember it on the news.

PAULINE   I was there for hours.
Until the dog-walkers and runners came, and
then the police, and then local groups. Then the
news crews. And then everyone else.

–

I found I couldn't leave.

–

They had these people putting wet towels over
them.
I asked one of them why it happened. How that
could happen?
When they already seen plain as day that they
were gonna die.
Why would they keep coming?
What happened to animal nature? Survival
instinct? Self-preservation??
And she said they don't know for sure.
But they have this theory.

–

Whales live in pods.
And they talk to each other. Communicate.

Travel all over the world all in these pods, these
families.
And they think that why it happens is
The first one goes by accident
Of course they don't know they're gonna get
into trouble
But then they call out to their family
Maybe they're saying 'I'm stuck, don't come
any closer, save yourselves!'
Maybe they're saying 'I'm stuck, help me! I'm
stuck, please help!'
Maybe it's 'I'm
I've found myself somewhere strange and I'm
alone
and I don't know what to do. I'm alone.'
But whatever it is they're saying
the rest of them follow.

RACHEL   Because that's what families do?

PAULINE   I'm your big sister and I'd always want for you
to save yourself but sometimes
Sometimes Rachel
it's felt to me like a stranding
and you've just swam away.

Seventeen

DAD	Little Miss Sunshine…
RACHEL	Dad!!!!!!!!!!!!!!!!
DAD	Ahhhhhhhhh hi mate. I missed you.
RACHEL	I didn't hear you you're SO SNEAKY
DAD	I think someone might have been asleep…
RACHEL	Not me.
DAD	No?
RACHEL	I've been waiting for you.
DAD	Oh really.
RACHEL	I've been waiting all day for you to get home but then Mum said that your aeroplane wasn't flying and so then maybe I went to bed.
DAD	I got another one.
RACHEL	When can I go on an aeroplane?
DAD	When we go on holiday.
RACHEL	But we always go on the canal.
DAD	You love the canal!
RACHEL	(*Sniffs him.*)
DAD	What you playing at little one??
RACHEL	Mum said you'll stink when you get home but you don't stink you smell nice.
DAD	Thanks baby. But she's right all that travelling. You should go to sleep and I should have a wash.
RACHEL	All that BEER.
DAD	–
	What?

RACHEL	Mum said that's the real reason the aeroplane didn't fly. Were you flying the aeroplane??
DAD	She said that?
RACHEL	She said that you were having beer with your friends.
DAD	Did she now.
RACHEL	I'm not cross Dad. You've just got loads of friends not like Mum. Mum's *boring*. When can I drink beer?
DAD	(*Laughs*.)
RACHEL	Where's my present?
DAD	Who says you're getting a present?
RACHEL	Dad!!!!
DAD	Okay okay it's in my bag Let me just

Eighteen

PAULINE	Hi Dad.
DAD	I was just getting your girls' presents.
PAULINE	Mum said you wouldn't be home tonight.
DAD	Yeah I've already heard what your mum's been saying.
PAULINE	–
DAD	Sorry.
PAULINE	How was it?
DAD	(*Makes a noise.*) Wish it'd have been Amsterdam ey. Then I could've bought you back a real present!
PAULINE	–
DAD	You're old enough for a brownie aren't you?
PAULINE	Dad that's weird.
DAD	Sorry Mary Poppins. Here you've not given your old man a hug yet.
PAULINE	–
DAD	I don't know what your mum's been saying
PAULINE	She's not said anything
DAD	while I've been working my arse off.
PAULINE	Dad…
DAD	You be careful Paul. You know there's nothing worse than a spiteful woman. That's a very poor example to be setting. – Here.
PAULINE	– What are they?

RACHEL	HEY NOT FAIR
DAD	Where did you come from!
RACHEL	Taking too long. I want mine too.
DAD	Here you go.
RACHEL	–
DAD	What's the matter?
PAULINE	What are they?
RACHEL	They're the same.
DAD	They're special biscuits, with caramel inside. You'll love them.
RACHEL	I wanted something different…
DAD	What did you want?
RACHEL	No different from *her*.
	–
DAD	Look they've got a stupid name. Stroop voffles. That's how they say it over there. Go on you try.
RACHEL	Stroop
PAULINE	Stroop waffles.
DAD	Voffles. Go on.
RACHEL	(*Giggles*.) Stroop voffles…
DAD	There she is. Now where's my thank-yous?
RACHEL	Thanks Dad.
PAULINE	Thanks Dad.
DAD	I'll get you something different next time. Something for my Mary Poppins. And something for my Little Miss Sunshine.

Nineteen

RACHEL   Would you like to see the messages?

PAULINE   Have you seen her?

RACHEL   No.
            Not yet.
            Would you want to come?

PAULINE   I don't think so.
            –
            She doesn't get to say goodbye to Dad.
            That's not how it works.

RACHEL   She said to say hi.

PAULINE   To me?

RACHEL   Yes.

PAULINE   What she said

RACHEL   'Hi to Pauline'

PAULINE   'Hi to Pauline'?

RACHEL   Yeah.

PAULINE   Like I'm the neighbour's daughter?

RACHEL   She's probably still scared of you.

PAULINE   Hardly.

RACHEL   I'm still pretty scared of you.

PAULINE   (*Makes a noise.*)

RACHEL   You're quite fearsome Paul.
            You're like a lion.
            Like a lioness.
            Around the people you love.

PAULINE   –

RACHEL   I always wished I could be more like that.
            Like you.

PAULINE   (*Makes a noise.*)

RACHEL   It's true.
             I did always want to be like you when I was little.

PAULINE   You wanted the exact opposite.

RACHEL   No I wanted to be distinctive.
             Because you were. Distinct.
             So wanting to be like you sort of meant
             Having to be the opposite.

PAULINE   –

RACHEL   It's really hard being sisters isn't it.
             I wonder if everyone finds it this hard.
             I wonder if it's always been this hard.

             –

PAULINE   I think maybe part of the problem is,
             is that when I talk to you I'm not really talking
             to you.

RACHEL   What d'you mean?

PAULINE   I'm talking to you at university
             and you at school
             and you at the hospital when I abandoned you
             to go on holiday with that
             dickhead
             and you as a teenager
             you as a kid, when you couldn't even tie your
             shoes.
             Sometimes it's really
             really
             hard, for me. To focus on the Rachel that's just
             standing in front of me right now.

             –

RACHEL   Paul?

PAULINE   Yep?

RACHEL   Thank you.

PAULINE   For what?

RACHEL   For everything.

Twenty

MUM   Are you ready to meet your sister?

               –

               What d'you think?

PAULINE   She's beautiful.

MUM   Isn't she.

PAULINE   She looks like you.

MUM   –
               D'you think?

PAULINE   I can't wait to play with her.

MUM   It'll be a while yet.

PAULINE   Horses and Barbies and cowboys like Calamity
               Jane
               And Victorian schools and ballet lessons and
               Top Trumps and Hide-and-Seek and races and
               Blocky 123
               And I'll teach her how to do plaits in her hair
               and
               We'll have a secret nightclub after you and Dad
               have gone to sleep with a password and
               everything
               And I'll show her how to make perfume out of
               water and petals and
               Mud pies and on the swing in the park and
               Pooh-Sticks down the river.
               And when I'm too old to actually play with her
               then I'll just set up the games for her and
               supervise.
               We'll do a play together for you at Christmas
               and
               Every birthday I'll make her something.

MUM   Today is her birthday. Her actual birth day.
               Day-of-her-birth birthday. Isn't that funny.
               –
               That all sounds like a lot of fun you're going to
               have together.

PAULINE	I forgot to make her something.
MUM	You didn't need to make her something.
PAULINE	Sorry.
MUM	I thought you might be jealous of a brand-new baby.
PAULINE	I'm not jealous. She's too small to be jealous of.
MUM	She'll get bigger.
PAULINE	When she's bigger we can be proper friends.
MUM	I hope so.
PAULINE	Are you okay Mummy? Does it hurt?
MUM	Just tired.
	–
	I'm sorry if I'm not always a perfect mum Pauline.
PAULINE	What colour's her hair gonna be like? Is it gonna be like mine? Can I see her open her eyes? Can we maybe just lift one a little bit?
MUM	We shouldn't wake her up.
PAULINE	No I'm not going to wake her up.
	–
MUM	Will you help me look after her?
PAULINE	Of course. That's my job. We're sisters.
MUM	Yes you are.
PAULINE	I'm going to love her forever. Forever and ever and ever. Do you hear me baby Rachel? You're my sister and I'll love you forever.

A Nick Hern Book

Daughterhood first published in Great Britain in 2019 as a paperback original by Nick Hern Books Limited, The Glasshouse, 49a Goldhawk Road, London W12 8QP, in association with Paines Plough and Theatr Clwyd

Daughterhood copyright © 2019 Charley Miles

Charley Miles has asserted her moral right to be identified as the author of this work

Cover design by Thread Design

Designed and typeset by Nick Hern Books, London
Printed in Great Britain by Mimeo Ltd, Huntingdon, Cambridgeshire PE29 6XX

A CIP catalogue record for this book is available from the British Library

ISBN 978 1 84842 883 6